Mental Toughness for Athletes

*7 Proven Strategies for Young Champions
to Build Grit, Boost Emotional
Resilience and Become Unstoppable*

AJ Kikumoto

ISBN 13 Paperback: 978-1-953556-21-9
ISBN 13 Hardback: 978-1-953556-22-6
ISBN 13 eBook: 978-1-953556-23-3
ISBN 13 Workbook: 978-1-953556-25-7

My husband Charles Kikumoto
Thank you for being our Super Disneyland Dad to our adorable children. You have stood by my side through every joy and hardship, and I am forever grateful for the remarkable person you are.

My Children Aaliyah, Akyra, Amaya, Akayla, CJ, and Alyvia
We are so very proud of you and your amazing accomplishments in ALL the sports!!! Thanks for inspiring me to write this book series.

My Parents
You are the foundation upon which my life was built, the unwavering support that has shaped my character and values. Your love, guidance, and sacrifices have paved the way for my success and instilled in me the importance of family, resilience, and compassion.

My Reader
I dedicate this book to you, the Reader.
You are ready to be mentally strong in this world. You can do hard things. You can and will change the world.

66

"I've missed more than 9000 shots in my career. I've lost almost 300 games. 26 times, I've been trusted to take the game winning shot and missed. I've failed over and over and over again in my life. And that is why I succeed."

~ Michael Jordan

CONTENTS

"A champion is someone who gets up when he can't."
~ Jack Dempsey, boxer

I was once a high school dancer who went on to become an NBA Denver Nugget Dancer. I learned that training my body and performing dance routines in my sleep wasn't enough. I had to train the one thing only the top 1% of athletes ever teach: the mindset muscle.

The wha-?

Former NFL wide receiver Trent Shelton says a championship mindset has five elements: commitment, discipline, consistency, faith, and heart. Basically, say yes, do the work, show up, believe in yourself, and give it everything.

But how do you put it all together?

How do you say yes when your mind says no? How do you sacrifice a typical high school social life for training? How do you push past failure or "not feeling it"? How do you develop belief in yourself when that little voice inside is saying you can't do this? How do you give it your all when you aren't sure you'll even succeed?

Developing that winner's attitude takes mental toughness.

But let me share a secret with you. I didn't torture myself to get to the top of my game. I didn't smother myself in shame when I messed up, and I messed up plenty. I embraced and laughed at the suck that is part of training and competition, and I learned how to become mentally tough. That's what I'm going to teach you here.

Take a sec to look back at your athletic career so far. How many times did you wonder if you were good enough? How many times did you fail and get discouraged... or fail and get back up, even more determined than before? How many times did you wonder why you're even doing this because it's going so badly... and then one small win completely turns things around?

Those are just a few examples of the mental game, which is the most important game you will play as an athlete and as a person.

Every athlete has, at one time or another, choked during competition. I'm going to show you how to never choke again.

Every athlete has psyched themselves out when learning a new skill. I will show you how to perform some incredible alchemy and turn fear into excitement.

Every athlete has struggled with discipline and heart when they're not on the winning side. I will show you how to love what you do even when nothing is going right.

I'm going to share the secrets of the champions with you.

You're about to take a fascinating and fun journey with two champion athletes, a runner named Abby and a swimmer named Luke, who will show you exactly what they did to have a winner's mindset.

I hope you laugh a little, learn a lot, and take this with you throughout your life.

What you're going to learn goes beyond any single sport. It applies to all sports and your life beyond sports.

I wish they taught mental toughness in school, but they don't, and the chances of having coaches throughout your athletic career that truly understand the power of the mind are pretty slim.

I believe that inside each of us is a genius and a champion. Who cares what other people say about your potential? I'm going to help you believe in yourself.

About Me

I am a former NBA Denver Nugget Dancer (Yay! World Champs!), CBA

Idaho Stampede Hot Shot Dancer, a professional backup dancer for bands and gigs, President of Boise State University Mane Line Dance team/national champion, high school dance coach, state and national champions, and professional model (FORD Chicago). Today, I am a mom of six beautiful children, five girls and one boy, who are all active in many sports. Football, dance, martial arts, basketball, volleyball, golf, tennis, lacrosse, and college dance are just a few examples of what my family is involved in and what my husband and I coach. My husband played college lacrosse and is a big sports enthusiast. I love my job as a dance instructor/coach at Starstruck Academy of Dance in Denver, Colorado. Beyond sports, I wear many other hats. One includes the free Uber driver hat, where I drive our kids to all their sports and activities. Another hat is the advocacy hat, where we work with the nonprofit Apraxia Kids, as four of our kids were born with Apraxia of Speech, a motor speech disorder that makes it difficult for children to speak. And, of course, many more hats, as that's what moms do!

Being a lifelong athlete has taught me many, many incredible lessons that I want to pass on to the next generation of young athletes — the young men and women who will shatter records and take every sport to the next level.

I am passionate about helping young high school athletes like you develop a winning mindset, including the mental toughness that will help you achieve any goal, no matter the challenges you face.

I hope that you will absolutely crush your athletic goals and that the mental toughness you build by reading this book and faithfully training your mindset muscle will help you succeed in anything: college, career, sport, and any goal you set for yourself.

Let's DO this!

Part 1 — The Toughness Game

Nobody participates in a sport because the sport is easy. We do it to challenge ourselves to reach higher. And it's not easy. Developing mental toughness will help you achieve your goals (and have more fun while at it) in sports and life in general.

"The higher you get, the harder it gets. That's life."

~ Adonis Creed, from the film Creed III

CHAPTER 1:

A CHAMPION'S MINDSET

"If you believe you can, you probably can. If you believe you won't, you most assuredly won't. Belief is the ignition switch that gets you off the launching pad."

~ Denis Waitley, motivational speaker/
author

In December of 2006, two-time adventure racing world champion and seven-time Ironman finisher Danielle Ballengee was out on a routine 8-mile training run outside of Moab, Utah, when she slipped on the ice and fell down an 80-foot cliff. She shattered her pelvis. Still conscious, Danielle knew the only way to save herself was to crawl. So she did.

Despite the unbearable pain and temperatures quickly dropping into the 20s, Danielle kept crawling. Five hours later, she had crawled a quarter of a mile. Her faithful dog Taz by her side, Danielle kept trying to stay awake and warm. Had she given in to sleep, she would have died of hypothermia.

More than 48 hours after her fall, the police located her car at the trailhead. As the search and rescue team started hiking in, Taz appeared. The dog refused to be caught, so the rescuers followed him. And Taz led them to Danielle.

Danielle had surgery to repair her shattered pelvis and spent 90 days in a wheelchair. Just 150 days after her horrific accident, Danielle was a fifth-place finisher in a 60-mile adventure race that featured running, orienteering, mountain biking, a ropes course, and kayaking.

Taz became an honored recipient of the National Hero Dog Award from the Society for the Prevention of Cruelty to Animals in Los Angeles.

What stands out in Danielle's story is not so much her amazing dog, who sped up the rescue effort... but Danielle's absolute refusal to quit. Despite her agonizingly painful injury, hypothermia, and exhaustion, Danielle persevered.

That is the mindset of a champion.

Mental toughness may seem to come easily to some people (and you're probably thinking, "not me, I wasn't born with it," — right?). You'll be glad to know that mental toughness is a learned skill.

Just like you learned and then mastered the physical aspects of your sport, you can learn and master the mental game.

What is Mental Toughness?
You can't pull mental toughness out of your gym bag

when your competition is ahead. It's not something you turn to with seconds left in the game.

Legendary ancient Greek athlete, Milo of Croton, was said to train by picking up a calf daily. Of course, calves grow fast, so Milo's training load was higher every day. He picked up and carried the growing bull until the animal reached its adult weight — or so the legend goes, since a full-grown bull can weigh upwards of a ton. But the point is that Milo lifted progressively heavier weights and became one of the most successful Olympic wrestlers of ancient times. It's not what he did during the competition that made him great. It's what he did relentlessly before the competition.

Mental toughness is what you do *before* you compete. What separates great athletes from good athletes of equal physical ability? It's not more squats or more intervals. It's not better nutrition or better equipment. It's mental toughness.

Mental toughness is the attitude that you are never "out of it." Even if you're in last place, *you have not lost* because you have given it everything. You compete with just as much heart whether you're

currently last or if you're currently in first, and *you never concede victory* until the race or event is over.

When you're mentally tough, you can handle setbacks and adversity without losing focus, confidence, or motivation. You can push past your limits of strength and endurance. You can doggedly practice a skill you're having trouble with, over and over and over again until you master it... *and then take that skill to the next level*. You can achieve your personal best in your weakest event or forget first-half mistakes and play as if everything hinges on the last second half. You can visualize success and remain laser-focused when everything is blowing up around you. You can access the Flow state (or "being in the Zone, a state of peak performance") in the face of distractions, disappointment, and conditions like bad weather, injury, pressure, pain, fatigue, or fear.

Mental toughness is your competitive edge. But the competition isn't "out there." The competition is you.

Meet Abby and Luke

Abby and Luke are inspiring high school athletes who will take you through the tenets of mental toughness.

You'll see where they started as high school athletes, what challenges they faced, how they overcame them, and how they developed unshakeable mental toughness.

Abby

Abby is a 16-year-old middle-distance runner specializing in the mile. She has always seen herself as an Olympian competing with the best in the world and someday shattering the record.

Abby's love for running was initially inspired by watching the Olympics and the incredible achievements of the top athletes. Record after record came down while Abby and her family sat glued to the screen, screaming for their favorites. Abby quickly discovered inspiration in Sifan Hassan, an Ethiopian-born middle- and long-distance runner who went from refugee to track superstar. Sifan and Abby share a birthday, January 1 — another reason for Abby to feel a bond with the Dutch athlete.

Sifan Hassan arrived in the Netherlands as a refugee in 2008. 15-year-old Sifan started running as a hobby. She soon fell in love with running and began competing. Sifan won three gold medals in the 2020 Tokyo Olympics (the only Olympic athlete to win both middle- and long-distance medals in a single Games. She is a three-time World Indoor Championships medalist, World Champion in the 1500m and 10,000m (where she held the 10,000m record for two days), European championship medalist, European record holder, and the 2020 one-hour run record holder.

Abby's older sisters are both competitive athletes. As the youngest of four, Abby was always chasing her sisters, hoping to catch up to them and be included in their games. As it turns out, Abby is naturally a fast runner, but it took watching the Olympics and the edge-of-your-seat excitement to inspire Abby to run competitively in high school.

At first, Abby was intimidated. While she was one of the lucky few who made varsity as a freshman, she immediately felt out of her league. Some of the other girls on the varsity team were good. SO good. Abby decided that the only way to get to their level was a lot of hard work, and she dove in without hesitation, putting 100% into every workout.

But what made the difference for Abby was not training her body; it was training her mind. She was inspired by Star Wars — the scene where Jedi master Yoda says, "Try not. Do or do not. There is no try." — when Luke Skywalker is complaining that he's trying but can't as he starts his Jedi training.

Abby started saying, in Yoda's raspy voice, of course, "Try not. Do or do not. There is no try." over and over whenever she felt unsure. Repeating this little mantra changed her attitude. She would no longer TRY her best; she would DO her best. "Trying" implies giving yourself permission to quit. "Doing" does not give you permission to quit. You are either doing it, or you aren't.

Luke

Luke is a 17-year-old swimmer. Luke grew up watching Michael Phelps become the most decorated Olympian ever with 28 medals... and a total combined 82 medals in the Olympics, Pan Pacific Championships, and World Championships. 65 of those medals were gold. Needless to say, Phelps wears size 14 shoes... those are big shoes to fill!

Luke's passion for swimming began as a toddler when his mom would spend summers at the community pool with Luke and his little sister. Luke wasn't what you consider a natural athlete. Tall, awkward, and not at all competitive as a kid, Luke just loved to be in the water. It wasn't until the 2012 London Olympics that Luke became fascinated with Phelps. Ironically, this was the year Phelps publicly stated he was "done with the sport" and intended to retire. Luke watched YouTube video after YouTube video of Phelps — nicknamed the Flying Fish or the Baltimore Bullet — completely dominating the 2008 Olympics. Luke expressed an interest in joining a swim team at age 10, and that's where his story started.

Luke wanted to emulate his hero, but try as he might, the Flying Fish's signature stroke, the butterfly, did not come easily for Luke. Something was missing. Ab work? Shoulder work? Luke tried it all and then by chance, he watched a TikTok where a man was doing some Tarzan-like moves, which turned out to be yoga. Luke noticed the man's incredible strength but also his flexibility and incredible fluidity of motion. A lightbulb went off in his head. Luke realized this was what he was missing.

Yoga could help him execute a more fluid and powerful stroke. Now, Luke had a plan.

Along with the time spent in the pool, Luke started taking yoga classes — with his classmates' moms. After the initial embarrassment of being the only high school kid in a room full of moms, Luke rose to the challenge. He was doing something his competitors weren't and this was going to give him the edge. He didn't realize at first how much yoga would train his mind in addition to his body. He became calmer and more focused. As his yoga improved, so did his swimming and his mindset. As his mindset improved, so did his times and his confidence. His success snowballed.

Journey along with Abby and Luke as they share their challenges and develop mental toughness.

CHAPTER 2

THE SCIENCE BEHIND MENTAL TOUGHNESS

"When it hurts to go, go faster."

~ Emil Zátopek, runner

Emil Zátopek was a Czech long-distance runner. The three-time gold medalist in the 1952 Helsinki Olympics (5,000m, 10,000m, and the marathon) was posthumously selected as the Greatest Runner of All Time by *Runner's World Magazine* in 2013.

His first two Helsinki medals were relatively straightforward for Zátopek. He was already a record holder in these distances. What blew people away was that he decided at the last minute to compete in the marathon. For the first time in his life. *At the Olympics.*

Emil was called the "Czech Locomotive" renowned for his incredibly brutal training methods. He was the runner who popularized interval training (you can thank him later). He would often run in work boots, in any weather, and sometimes even with his wife, Dana, riding piggyback.

But let's back up to his teen years. As a 16-year-old working in a shoe factory, Zátopek recalls how the factory sports coach (a very strict man) selected four boys, including Zátopek, to run in a race. Zátopek protested but was ordered to run anyway. When the race started, Zátopek realized that this was fun, and he wanted to win. He "only" came in second... out of 100. But the fire was lit. He joined a local sports club and lacking a coach, he developed his own rigorous training program.

Four months later, he was already shattering records. After a mandatory stint in the Czechoslovak Army, he was selected for the Czechoslovak national team and participated in the 1948 Olympics, where he won a silver and a gold. For the next few years, he continued to break record after record.

In the 1952 Olympics, his 5,000m victory was a nail-biter to the end. In fourth place at the start of the fourth and final lap, Zátopek turned on the afterburners and surged ahead to win the gold medal. And then on a whim he went and signed up for the Olympic marathon.

His marathon strategy was very simple: stick with the guy in the lead. This didn't sit well with "the guy in the lead," British world record-holder Jim Peters. 15k into the race, Peters was already struggling to shake his pursuer. Zátopek asked Peters what he thought of the race so far, whether he was enjoying himself, and so on. Peters was shocked at this relaxed chit-chat and replied that the pace was "too slow," hoping to psych out his opponent. Zátopek nodded and accelerated. He surged past Peters and took a commanding lead. Peters was unable to finish. Zátopek won the race. Oh, and he also set a new Olympic record.

Zátopek's running style was often painful to watch. He looked as though every step was pure agony, his face contorted, wheezing heavily, head rolling to the side... one spectator said that Zátopek resembled "a man wrestling with an octopus on a conveyor belt." An *Athletics Weekly* reporter said, "He ran as only Zátopek could run such a distance, one moment looking like a super-tuned machine, the next like a fugitive from justice; grimacing painfully in one lap, smiling contentedly in the next, and finally winding up with a last lap that would have done credit to a first-class miler."

So what was behind the Czech Locomotive's 18 world records, 5 Olympic medals (4 gold), and his spontaneous entry and victory in the 1952 Olympic marathon? Interval training, for one. You may think that Zátopek was naturally fast, but he wasn't. His interval training was solely aimed at increasing his speed. Now, keep in mind that his training program was not high-tech like today: no heart rate monitors, no coaches with stopwatches, and no VO2 max indicators. Zátopek simply ran intuitively by feel. He varied his effort based on what he thought was right.

Zátopek personifies true grit. He is considered a true innovator in developing mental toughness. Here's a peek into his psyche:

- "Pain is a merciful thing. If it lasts without interruption, it dulls itself."
- When criticized for his running style, he snapped back, "I shall learn to have a better style once they start judging races according to their beauty."
- When doing insanely high-volume interval training (in army boots) in snow and mud, people were shocked. He remembers them saying, "Emil, you're a fool!" But as soon as he won the European Championship for the first time, suddenly it was, "Emil, you're a genius!"
- "There is a great advantage in training under unfavorable conditions... for the difference is then a tremendous relief in a race."
- "It's at the borders of pain and suffering that the men are separated from the boys."

- "When a person trains once, nothing happens. When a person forces himself to do a thing a hundred or a thousand times, then he certainly develops in ways more than physical. Is it raining? That doesn't matter. Am I tired? That doesn't matter either. Willpower becomes no longer a problem."
- "When it hurts to go, go faster."

One hint at Zátopek's toughness comes from his overall attitude. You see, running, and pushing his body past its limits, was fun. And we all know that when we're having fun, we can go so much harder than we can when we hate life. Zátopek was an incredibly happy, enthusiastic, and generous man. When he offered advice to other runners, he would counsel them to gently touch the thumb with the tip of the index or middle finger as a reminder to relax the arms.

Sports Psychology

"Listen to Duke!" ~ Adonis Creed to Damian, about listening to the coach, from the film Creed III

Sports psychology is the science behind mental toughness. It draws on understanding how the human mind works and techniques like meditation to train the mind. It's the study of motivation and developing self-awareness and self-mastery.

In 1898, psychologist Norman Triplett was the first to conduct an experiment relating to sports psychology. His research showed that the physical presence of competitors made cyclists race faster in group races than in individual time trials. This research sparked interest in what makes some athletes consistent winners while others or equal physical ability are consistently just off the podium or don't make it past the semi-finals.

Back then, mental toughness was called a "can do" attitude and was considered closely tied to discipline. It was believed that the more disciplined you become, the tougher you will be. That's true. But what makes you more disciplined? Here's where sports psychology comes in with an understanding of motivation: what makes you want to become more disciplined?

It wasn't until the 1960s that sports psychology became popular. Immediately, professional athletes and coaches took notice. Coach Vince Lombardi (active in the 1960s) is one of the most famous NFL coaches in history, and much of his success is attributed to developing mental toughness in his players.

He said, "Winning isn't everything; it's the only thing."

In the 1980s, the U.S. Olympic Committee assembled a registry of sports psychologists to support athletes who wanted to improve their mental game.

Today, many coaches regularly evaluate their athletes and help them overcome challenges. The hallmarks of mentally tough athletes include sportsmanship, resiliency, courage, ethics, determination, flexibility, and adaptability.

When hundredths of seconds matter as the difference between first and fourth, remember the words of American sports psychologist Dr. Jim Loehr of the Human Performance Institute. He defines mental toughness as "the ability to consistently perform towards the upper range of your talent and skill regardless of competitive circumstances."

Thankfully today, some really cool psychological tricks make it fun to develop mental toughness. Once you understand these mind hacks, you can use them on yourself.

Abby and Luke both take inspiration from the greats who came before them. And not just in their sport!

Abby's cousins are all big football players, and she has picked up the love of football from them. She knows the teams and players. She reads up on the big achievers. From her perspective as an athlete, she can see when players choke in a game. She can see when they struggle to hold it together and refuse to lie down and quit, even in the face of a shutout.

Luke has recently become interested in Leo Urban (the "French Tarzan"), an athlete who leaps from tree to tree, barefoot and without gloves, with incredible grace and strength. The mental toughness of this guy is legendary. Ever since Luke saw Urban for the first time on YouTube, he has been fascinated with what it takes mentally to perform stunts like this.

CHAPTER 3

STARTING POINTS

> **"If you can imagine it, you can achieve it. If you can dream it, you can become it."**
>
> ~ William Arthur Ward, writer

All elite athletes will agree that whatever your sport — whether it's an individual sport or a team sport — *you win or you lose because of what's going on between your ears.*

Top athletes are often seen as exceptional, and they are, but watching your favorites win time after time after time gets kind of boring. What makes watching the champions so compelling isn't watching them win but watching them win by a fraction of a second or bounce back after a terrible season or serious injury.

Let's dive into the characteristics of mental toughness, starting with a non-judgmental self-assessment. Check-in with yourself honestly and note which of these you're good at and which you're struggling with.

One of the best things you can do to hard-wire the concepts in this book into your brain is to complete the companion guide Workbook to this book. Consider it a powerful part of your training!

What's Your Level of Mental Toughness Right Now?

Read through the following characteristics of a mentally tough athlete. Do an honest assessment of what you're good at and where you need some help. This is your starting point.

Don't give yourself a hard time if your scores are not great. Your mission is to improve, not to immediately achieve a perfect score in every element of mental toughness. You'll get there!

Do You Have a Winner's Mindset?

A winner's mindset is the unshakeable belief that you will do your very best no matter what and have what it takes to win. You are confident in your abilities, but you are not arrogant and assume that you *will* win.

You pursue excellence and improvement, not perfection. You are not embarrassed by mistakes or losses. You push yourself to be better. When things don't go as planned, you don't crumble; you learn from it.

You value developing your skills and talents. You don't resent other athletes' successes; you celebrate them and learn from them.

On a scale of 1 to 3, honestly assess yourself on your winner's mindset.

- 1 = I need more confidence here.
- 2 = Sometimes. Working on it.
- 3 = "I got this."

Abby and Luke both scored a 2. This might surprise you, given their accomplishments! They both admit to still being intimidated by other athletes, which erodes their self-confidence. They both say, "I'm working on it!" — *Usually*, they can rally and regain their focus before an event.

Life Hack
Beyond sports, a winner's mindset will give you the confidence to live the life you want. You'll have the confidence to pursue any career you want, even if it goes against what everyone thinks is right for you.

Are You Mentally Prepared?
You have mentally rehearsed the potential positive outcomes. This inspires and motivates you. You have mentally rehearsed the potential negative outcomes.

This helps you formulate a backup plan and be more resilient if things don't go how you want.

Mental preparedness helps you trust your training and do what you need to do, whatever the circumstances. It helps you recover quickly and continue with your performance without letting it affect your focus.

Most of all, mental preparedness takes away the fear of failure. You've already rehearsed what it's like to succeed and to fail. If you fail, okay. You learn and move forward, more experienced and stronger.

On a scale of 1 to 3, honestly assess your mental preparedness.

- 1 = I need more confidence here.
- 2 = Sometimes. Working on it.
- 3 = "I got this."

Abby scored a 2 — she's still struggling with some things that a few "mean girls" said to her.

Luke scored a 3. His hero, Michael Phelps, was the inspiration for learning how to rehearse every possible scenario mentally.

<u>Life Hack</u>
Beyond sports, being mentally prepared will help you adapt quickly and make smarter decisions because you will have already rehearsed what you could do if things go perfectly and what you could do if things go wrong. You'll have a Plan B for every weird contingency you can think of. If the totally unexpected happens, you're confident you'll figure it out.

Do You Remain Hyper-Focused?

You know how to get into the Zone. You know how to trust your training and tune out external and internal distractions like the haters and doubters, as well as your fears, doubts, and anxiety.

You focus on what you can control: *you*. You don't waste energy worrying about what you can't control. You focus on what you can in the situation.

On a scale of 1 to 3, honestly assess yourself on your level of focus when faced with inner and outer distractions.

- 1 = I need more confidence here.
- 2 = Sometimes. Working on it.
- 3 = "I got this."

Abby and Luke both scored 2. Sometimes, the noise of spectators during competition gets to them since it's very different from training in a quiet track or pool.

Life Hack
Beyond sports, the ability to remain focused will help you in school and in business. You won't let insignificant stuff distract you from learning, from your goals, or from creativity.

How Well Do You Manage Stress?
You don't choke in competition. You don't cave because of the pressure your coach, school, or parents put on you. You transform fear into excitement. You know how to stay in the Zone even during setbacks such as falls or missed shots. You *never* give up, even if you're currently in last place. You continue to give your best no matter what.

Olympic swimmer Matt Biondi was an overwhelming favorite to win 7 Gold medals at the 1988 Olympic games. That's a lot of pressure! Matt lost his first two finals; some athletes would have mentally quit right there and not given their best in the remaining five events. Not Matt. Matt managed the stress of losing and letting down his fans, his coach, his team, his country... *everybody*, including himself... and ended up winning five Gold medals in the '88 games.

On a scale of 1 to 3, honestly assess your ability to manage stress.

- 1 = I need more confidence here.
- 2 = Sometimes. Working on it.
- 3 = "I got this."

Abby scores a 2 on this. Her go-to before competition is to *have more fun than her competitors*. As you'll see later, this is an incredible superpower! Luke scored a 2 because he doesn't want to disappoint anyone. Sometimes, it gets to him.

Life Hack
Beyond sports, managing stress will help you make better choices. You won't react to problems... you'll respond to them calmly and wisely.

How Well Do You Break Through Limits?

You know that your limits are temporary and, in many cases, self-imposed. You love to push the boundaries of what you can do. You can perform despite the pain, fatigue, and negative self-talk. You know that if you did something once, you can do it again and better. You also know that where you are now is not "it." You can always push a little harder.

However, when you're mentally tough, you also take excellent care of your body. Some people think mentally tough athletes will push through the pain no matter what and end up injured, overtrained, and burned out. That is *not* what happens to an athlete who has developed mental toughness because a mentally tough athlete recognizes that rest is part of training and that they can use downtime from injury to work on other aspects of their sport... Like mental toughness!

When you continually push your limits, you adapt and get better. Instead of doing things as you've always done, you find new ways of challenging yourself. You know what you did yesterday got you here... but it won't get you to the next level.

On a scale of 1 to 3, honestly assess your ability to push past your limits.

- 1 = I need more confidence here.
- 2 = Sometimes. Working on it.
- 3 = "I got this."

Both Abby and Luke scored a 3 here. They both love to say something like, "Oh yeah? Watch me!" when someone or their own doubts say, "You can't do this."

Life Hack
Beyond sports, pushing your limits and moving beyond them (which translates to moving beyond your fears) will let you achieve *anything* you set your mind to. Period.

How Resilient Are You?
You find a way, not an excuse. You don't play the victim when things don't go your way. You don't play the blame game. You own your performance. You persevere.

You don't fail; you learn. You know you *fail* only when you don't get up and try again. You know that "failures" and "mistakes" are simply lessons in how to do things better next time. You don't fear failure because you know it's a necessary step to getting to the next level.

You take risks knowing that you might not win. You actively seek out opportunities to push out of your comfort zone. You meet all challenges with enthusiasm, not dread or anxiety.

Most of all, knowing how to fail well makes your sport more fun. Who cares if you "failed" or lost or made a mistake? Seeing failure as a step towards personal excellence takes the pressure off and makes it fun to train and compete.

On a scale of 1 to 3, honestly assess your ability to bounce back.

- 1 = I need more confidence here.
- 2 = Sometimes. Working on it.
- 3 = "I got this."

Abby remembers scoring a 1 in resilience when she first started mental toughness training. Now, she's a confident 3. Luke says he's a 3 but will admit that sometimes he beats himself up for failures because he *knows* he could have done better.

Life Hack

Beyond sports, failing well will help you take smart risks. You won't be afraid to fail, so you'll go where your peers are too afraid to go. You will succeed in life because you're not afraid to live it.

YOUR Starting Point

"Champs gotta start somewhere, right?" ~ Adonis Creed, from the film Creed III

Wherever you are, don't compare yourself to others. Everyone is good at different things. Only focus on what you need to improve within yourself.

Write your answers in the companion guide Workbook and put a date there. Go back next month, and next year, after you've been practicing mental toughness and reassess your score. *Your mission is to improve, not to immediately achieve a perfect score in every element of mental toughness.*

Your Mind Is Your Competitive Edge

Remember, your talent and all those hours of training and perfecting techniques will get you close, but *they won't get you there first.*

Now you know how your mindset determines athletic success. It determines

- How much energy you're going to have on game day
- Whether you give 100% or 99.99%
- Whether you persevere and stay motivated in the face of massive suck
- Whether you let a defeat ruin your season or you rise up wiser and stronger
- *Whether you stay in love with your sport*

In this chapter you learned what mental toughness is and how it translates into sports and life. I hope you see yourself in some of the examples.

I also hope that you can see that by developing mental toughness, you will overcome any obstacles in your way.

Part 2 – The 7 Proven Strategies of Becoming Unstoppable

"The battle is between your ears."
~ Joey McGuire, Texas Tech head football coach

If only we could just swipe up and enter a dimension where our mind never lets us down. But we aren't there yet, so for now, we have to do it the old-fashioned way.

Before we get too deep into the book, I want to say one thing: sports should be fun. I grew up in an era where coaches often yelled at athletes in the name of motivation. Yeah, yeah, I walked sixteen miles to school each way, barefoot, in blizzards, uphill both ways, in the dark, carrying eighty pounds of books... and I liked it. See? That's the world's first example of mental toughness!

But in all seriousness...

Back then, it was believed that mental toughness had to be drilled into you. I actually had one coach scream at me, "Pain is weakness leaving the body!" which really did not help my attitude because my first thought in response to that was, "Why am I doing this?"

Let's introduce mental toughness in a much more excellent way, with the 7 proven strategies for becoming unstoppable.

CHAPTER 4

STRATEGY #1 OF BEING UNSTOPPABLE — SET THE RIGHT GOALS

"I can't think of anyone I admire who isn't fueled by self-doubt. It's an essential ingredient. It's the grit in the oyster."

~ Richard Eyre, Film Director

Goals are there to help you manage self-doubt. Just as an oyster needs a bit of grit or debris in the shell to form a pearl, you need self-doubt to fuel you. That's right! You need to doubt that you can so that you can PROVE you can.

That's where goals come in.

From the first time you lace up your skates or pull on your helmet, you're setting goals that continue to get bigger and more challenging as your skills improve.

Before you achieve goals, you have to set them. Even Emil Zátopek's last-minute decision to compete in the Olympic marathon was a goal. Did he intend to win it or just see what he was capable of? The point is he set a goal for himself and did what he needed to do to achieve it.

Goals motivate you, improve your performance, help you focus on your priorities, and give you confidence and a sense of control.

Take a moment to write down your top 3 athletic goals. Don't worry about how big or small they are or how achievable you think they are. Just write them down.

I'm going to show you how to achieve these goals.

The Art of Goal-Setting

"I'm gonna get there one day. I'm gonna get there." ~
Adonis Creed, from the film Creed III

There is an art to setting goals. It's called SMART.

SMART goals can be outcome goals, process goals, and performance goals.

- Outcome goals are the end result: making the team; the championship; medals; a PR (personal record)
- Process goals are the milestones by which you measure progress
- Performance goals are the personal level of mastery you wish to achieve: a specific mile time, a specific skill, etc.

SMART goals are:

Specific

Choose a specific outcome you want to achieve: winning the State Championship, shaving 20 seconds off your time, mastering a specific balance beam mount, etc. Too vague goals, like "get better at backflips," are harder to achieve because they're boring. Your specific goals should excite you! Write your specific goal in your Workbook.

Abby's next specific goal is to shave 3 seconds off her 500m time. Luke's next specific goal is to beat his top rival more consistently, even if it's by 1/100th of a second.

Measurable

Measurable goals, such as tracking your time improvements in sprints, are incredibly motivational. Use your Workbook as a training log where you monitor your progress. What's working? What's not working? Where do you need to put in the extra effort? Where do you need to change your strategy and adapt to different situations?

Abby and Luke both love to track their progress. Any time they make progress, they keep pushing. Whenever they reach a plateau, they add something different to their training. Sometimes mixing things up is enough to hit the "refresh" button in the brain!

Actionable

Define specific steps to achieve this goal. Take climbing a mountain as a metaphor. Standing at the bottom looking up, it's huge and intimidating. Break it up into actionable steps that aren't overwhelming. You can take any huge goal and break it down into monthly, then weekly, then daily goals. Now you have a daily plan for climbing the biggest mountain. In your workbook, write down what actionable DAILY steps you will take to achieve weekly, monthly, and bigger goals.

Abby and Luke have worked with their coaches to develop a daily training plan (including rest days) that works on power, speed, and endurance.

Realistic

Above all, you must *believe* that you can achieve it. A goal should be *temporarily* out of reach. Too big, and you become overwhelmed and will likely quit. Too small, and you get bored and lose motivation. If a goal is too ambitious, break it down into reasonable goals that you know you can achieve with a little extra effort. Once you achieve it, set another slightly bigger goal and then another. Write your realistic goal in your Workbook.

Abby often bites off more than she can chew. She has learned to chunk her goals into steps she can actually accomplish every day. Even if these steps are still uncomfortable, they're manageable. Luke finds that he constantly has to adjust his goals. Sometimes they'll be too hard, and he'll lose motivation. Sometimes, they're too easy. He says, "As long as it's a *little* hard, you can do it."

Timely

It's hard to balance school, training, and even work, but consistently working on your daily goals is magic. Use the workbook to write out timely goals following these guidelines:

- Set *a reasonable hard deadline* by which you want to achieve this goal. Don't put it so far out in the future that you forget about it or lose motivation.
- Keep in mind *how much time you realistically have* to achieve this goal by your deadline and what you can do to carve out more time in your day. You may need to set smaller goals that fit within your

time constraints and work up to the bigger ones.
- *Reward yourself at the end of the week!* Movie night? Hanging out with friends? A hot bubble bath?
- *Give yourself consequences at the end of the week for NOT sticking to your daily goals.* 2-3 minute cold showers? No TV?

 Both Abby and Luke have a much more regimented day than most high school athletes. They have made some hard sacrifices. Abby likes to reward herself with a Netflix night at the end of the week, and Luke takes a luxurious day completely off, on the couch, doing absolutely nothing, every Sunday.

Reverse-Engineer Your Goals

"Doubt kills more dreams than failure ever will."

~ *Suzy Kassem, poet*

A dream is big. And intimidating. But you can break any dream into milestones or smaller goals. Success at achieving any gigantic goal involves breaking down big goals into micro-goals or daily steps you can take daily. It really is that simple.

Luke

Luke's ultimate goal used to be: to beat Michael Phelps' record in the 200m butterfly. He knew this massive goal wouldn't be achieved during high school. Instead of getting frustrated, Luke focuses on steady improvements to get him to the top of collegiate swimming and the Olympics.

But, as records tend to do, they fall, and the bar is set just a little higher. In July 2019, Hungarian swimmer Kristóf Milák broke Phelps' record by a little more than 2/10 of a second. And then Milak broke his own record in June 2022 by yet another 2/10 of a second.

Luke cheerfully laughs and says, "Bring it!" because he knows that if he sticks to the plan and focuses on steady improvement, he will have a shot at the record.

Abby

Abby is, quite honestly, not a fan of rigorous training methods where everything is measured. She prefers to run intuitively, pushing herself when she feels good and taking things back a notch when she feels overtrained or off. But, she respects the progress that she has made because of her ability to regularly set challenging goals for herself. She knows that keeping a training log and tracking her progress proves that it works, and she is very, very motivated by even the tiniest improvement.

Set Small Goals for Every Day

Achieving small goals daily is a testament to your self-discipline. Challenge yourself to set 5 small daily goals that will move you in the right direction. Here are some ideas:

- Make your bed
- Homework before scrolling
- Name 10 things you're grateful for
- Arrive 10 minutes early for practice, and mentally rehearse mastering a move or technique
- Choose plain water over soft drinks
- Choose a healthy snack over junk food
- Read 10 pages
- Plank for 1 minute

5 small goals achieved every day equal 150 small goals in a month and 1800 goals in a year. That's momentum!

Set Consequences for Not Meeting Your Goals

99% of the time, we don't achieve goals because of actions we didn't take, choices we made, and so on. So when you're looking at those small daily goals that you know you can achieve and yet choose not to... give yourself a consequence! Sometimes, negative consequences are just as motivating as positive rewards. My favorite consequence? A 2-minute cold shower!

Dealing with Setbacks

"When we tackle obstacles, we find hidden reserves of courage and resilience we did not know we had. And it is only when we are faced with failure do we realise that these resources were always there within us."
~ A. P. J. Abdul Kalam, aerospace scientist and former president of India

What about setbacks to achieving your goals? Every athlete faces obstacles and setbacks like losses or injuries. That's where breaking down goals into smaller goals, down to the "daily actions" level, and something unwanted happens that sets you back; you just pick up the program *wherever you are* once you're ready to start again.

Mental rehearsal, another word for deliberate visualization (we'll talk about this later), is something you can do when you're injured. You can help prevent losing muscle strength while injured with mental rehearsal. In an interesting study, researchers wanted to determine if you could increase muscle strength just by visualizing a movement. The answer was yes. Group 1 performed physical finger contractions, and Group 2 performed "mental contractions." Both groups did these exercises for 15 minutes a day, 5 days a week, for 12 weeks. As expected, the physical training group increased finger strength by 53%. But the "mental contractions" group also saw 35% improvement in strength, literally without lifting a finger. This really demonstrates the power of the mind!

Abby

Abby suffered a devastating setback as a sophomore runner, with severe plantar fasciitis pain that kept her off the track for over a month, right in the middle of the season. She switched gears and hopped on her mom's road bike, mostly on the trainer but also out on the open roads. Cross-training kept her fitness high without aggravating her foot pain. She even saw improvements in strength from cycling. While she was upset to miss several key meets, she was not about to let plantar fasciitis crush her dreams. Between cycling, strength training, and visualization, Abby made the best use of her downtime and came back absolutely on fire in her junior year.

Luke

Luke struggled with a series of embarrassing losses in a key swim meet in his junior year, just one week after breaking up with his girlfriend. He couldn't focus, he was depressed, he wasn't eating, he had no energy to work out, and he felt like his whole existence was worthless. This meet was important because it was the one that could qualify his school for the state championships. The rest of the team performed well and barely qualified for the semis, but Luke's dismal performance sent him into a brief tailspin. His coach took Luke aside before practice and handed him a sheet of paper. At first, Luke was sure he was being kicked off the team, but to his surprise, on the paper was a long list of Luke's accomplishments. Win after win after win. "Don't let one bad day ruin your life," said the coach.

"Remember what Jack Dempsey said, 'A champion is someone who gets up when he can't. Take a week off, and let's focus on State. I want you there. The team wants you there. I don't expect you to get over this in a week or anything like that. Just channel that energy into something good for you."

Once you have the right mindset, setbacks won't be such a catastrophe, and we'll develop your mindset next; setbacks can become powerful motivators. "What doesn't kill you makes you stronger," right?

CHAPTER 5

STRATEGY #2 OF BEING UNSTOPPABLE — DEVELOP MOTIVATION IN ANY SITUATION

> **"If you want to be the best, you can't take the path of least resistance. Every morning, you wake up, and your mind tells you it's too early, and your body tells you you're a little too sore, but you've got to look deep within yourself and know what you want and what you're striving for."**
>
> ~Antonio Brown, football player

Sports are hard. Training can be brutal both physically and mentally. Not everyone can be a winner. So how do you maintain motivation when the going gets tough?

It's 5 AM on a Saturday. It's 35 degrees and pouring rain. The alarm screams in your ear. Groaning, you smash the snooze button and pull the covers over your head. For a moment, you lie there wishing you didn't have to leave your warm cozy bed to show up at the track for a meet.

A winner will stop whining as quickly as the whining starts (it will start, but a winner knows how to shut it down). A winner will just get up and get ready, focused ahead on the challenge of today's meet. They never lose sight of their goal.

Everyone else will procrastinate until the last minute, begging for "just 5 more minutes." They show up at the track grudgingly, already in a bad mood that seems to sap their energy. They go through the motions without enthusiasm.

What do *you* do?

Chances are you've been in both situations.

A few psychological mind hacks help you stay motivated even when the universe seems to be conspiring against showing up and doing the work.

Your Why

Do you know your Why? Why are you competing in this sport? Why do you want to be really, really good at it? Why do you want to win? What drives you to succeed? To train? To compete? To stick with it when you really don't want to? If you aren't motivated by a strong Why, you won't commit, give your best, persevere, or bounce back from adversity.

Here's a glimpse into what motivates Luke and Abby.

Luke *loves* competition. He gets a lot of inspiration from seeing his competitors in the lanes next to his. The mere sight of them drives him to greater efforts.

Abby recalls pushing herself to a personal best only because she caught a glimpse, out of the corner of her eye, of another runner slowly gaining on her. Abby is "hungry." She approaches every meet with an insatiable hunger to push past her own personal best. Luke saw good success in swim meets almost from the beginning. He's used to winning, so he doesn't feel as hungry to win as Abby does. Luke and Abby both come from relatively privileged backgrounds. However, some kids on their teams have to balance training with work and school work. Both Luke and Abby have taken note of the bulldog-like tenacity of kids who want to prove to the world that they can do it. Those kids are hungrier for the win than most anybody.

Luke and Abby have both suffered enough defeats to know it's not the end of the world. They still have some anxiety about competing against athletes who have beaten them in the past, but they remain focused, and both take the simple attitude of having fun and doing their best. Luke *knows* he is capable of winning because he has done it before. He also knows that winning is not a given and that too much self-confidence could make him complacent. He trusts that in the heat of the moment, he has what it takes to win the race, and if he doesn't, then he'll be hungrier next time.

Abby expects to have fun. She has found that when she puts too much pressure on herself to win, she doesn't enjoy the meet and often doesn't do well. But when she decides to have fun and let her feet fly... that's a different story, and it usually ends with her having a blast and medaling.

Both Luke and Abby enjoy winning and the prizes that come with it, but they are more driven by personal pride in accomplishment.

The Art of Self-Motivation

"Hard days are the best because that's when champions are made."
~ Gabby Douglas, gymnast

Olga Chusovitina is a gymnast from Uzbekistan. Where many elite athletes retire in their 30s, Chusovitina, now 47, has competed in eight Olympic games (the only gymnast ever), 16 World Championships, 4 Asian Games, and 3 Goodwill Games. Her career has spanned more than three decades. She announced her retirement in 2012 but returned to competition immediately afterward, and she plans on qualifying for the 2024 Olympics in Paris. According to her coach, she spends more time on mental preparation and visualization now than on the physical aspects of her specialty, the vault. What's remarkable about Chusovitina is not so much that she has been able to maintain the physical ability to compete at the highest level but that she has kept her passion alive for so many years.

Your Why is going to drive you. Even the promise of a medal or a championship ring may not be enough to get you to suffer as much as you need to suffer sometimes. You have to know what drives you deep inside, as Chusovitina has consistently done for over three decades.

Behind motivation lies one common theme: *how you feel when you accomplish a goal*.

Your Why isn't to win a medal. You got a shiny prize, *but how do you feel?* Your Why isn't to set a new personal best. Great achievement, but *how do you feel?* Your Why isn't for your team to win Nationals. Everybody calls you heroes, but how do you feel? Your Why isn't to make the Olympic team. Awesome! *How do you feel?*

You see, WHY you want to succeed or win is really because *you want to feel a certain way.*

Close your eyes and imagine the point of achieving your biggest athletic goal. FEEL it. Do you feel pride? Satisfaction? Relief? Whatever you feel that you want to feel, **that's your Why**, and that's what's going to drive you.

Both Luke and Abby enjoy receiving medals, but both admit that the medals are secondary. It's how they *feel* about themselves when they receive those medals that really matters.

Keeping the Fire Alive

Looking at athletes you admire, it's easy to see their accomplishments and forget they're human too. The stress of competition, especially at the elite level, can take its toll on those who aren't mentally tough. Some lose the desire to compete, while others find ways to keep the fire alive and stay in love with their sport.

Triathlete Sophie Kirk struggled with anxiety that led to her questioning whether she even wanted to compete anymore. In 2020, she pulled out of a major event for several reasons. First, she couldn't get her head in the game after a summer of no competition due to COVID-19. She couldn't sleep and became hyper-focused on the stress of competition. She also didn't want to be around masses of people and didn't feel physically prepared for the competition.

While pulling out of the race felt right at the time, Sophie began wondering if she even wanted to race again. She had always said that she loved racing, pre-race nerves and all, but now the thought of racing was causing more and more anxiety.

Sophie decided to tone things down by entering a local 10-mile Tuesday Night Time Trial — a far cry from the elite-level races she was used to. She experienced the same pre-race anxiety, but because it was a small local race and she had no expectations, she made herself start. As soon as she was on the course, something inside her clicked, and she was back to loving competition.

Sophie Kirk became a triathlete in 2015. She is currently a two-time Ironman 70.3 World Championship qualifier and has podiumed at every 70.3 event she has competed in.

Did you know that Michael Phelps was diagnosed with ADHD at age 9? Swimming helped keep Phelps focused and developed discipline, and those are some of the reasons his mom urged him to swim. Later in his career, Phelps struggled with depression and alcohol abuse. He is now an advocate for mental health awareness. He said, "That's scary as hell... Thinking about taking your own life, I remember sitting in my room for four or five days, not wanting to be alive, not talking to anybody. That was a struggle for me ... I reached that point where I finally realized I couldn't do it alone... I want to be able to get out in front and talk and say, 'Look, yes, I've done these great things in the pool, but I'm also a human. I'm also a human like some people in this world who are going through the same exact struggles that I have... I want people to understand that there are times that you will have to reach out."

Athletes are often seen as having high degrees of obsessive perfectionism to the point that a second-place finish is a horrible failure. Margaux Isaksen is a modern pentathlete and three-time Olympian. She finished fourth at the London Olympics in 2012, just off the podium. "I just remember thinking, wow, if I had run a second faster or got one extra fencing touch, then I would have a medal. And I just came home and felt so defeated and sad..." she said. She finished 20th at the Rio Olympics in 2016, sending her into a tailspin of depression. "It makes you feel sort of worthless. It's a powerful word, but that's kind of how I feel right now. I really feel like I've let myself down, let my coaches down, and that's hard. And then you don't know if you want to put yourself through that again."

Please seek help if you feel that the pressure of competition weighs so heavy on you that it sucks all the joy out of the sport. Asking for help is NOT a sign of weakness. It's a sign of immense courage.

If you need help NOW, please call 988 (suicide and crisis hotline) or 1800-273-8255 (national suicide prevention hotline).

Humor

Luke's older brother is an ultra-distance cyclist. He regularly trains for 4-5 hours at a time and competes in 100-mile, 24-hour, and multi-day road and mountain bike races. He'll be the first to tell you that about 50 miles into a 100-mile race, he wishes he never got on the bike that morning. In fact he wishes he had never taken up the sport. He asks himself why he spent money to do something this stupid, *on purpose*? He starts to laugh at the absurdity of it all: crossing miles and miles of countryside on 1" wide tires, under his own power, on a saddle that feels about as comfy as a slab of granite, swallowing the occasional bug, alone in the heat and the wind... and somehow, laughing about it takes his mind off the suck. By 80 miles into it, he has forgotten the mid-race "death march," and his mind is firmly on the finish line just 20 miles away. At that point, there's no point in quitting. *Just push harder, Adam, get it over with, and go have a massage!*

As an athlete, you're putting yourself in challenging situations that will test you. Humor can get you out of the worst mental funk, especially if you can laugh at the absurdity of doing this on purpose!

Use humor as often as you can. Being too serious can lead to negative thoughts, which, as you know, feed fear and make you weak. Humor, on the other hand, leads to positive thoughts that feed courage and energize and strengthen you.

Smile through the pain. Holding a smile for just two minutes signals to your brain that life is good, everything is okay, no reason to panic or stop having fun. You can actually raise your pain threshold by smiling through it. If the smile is more like a grimace, just hold it and see what happens!

Embrace the Challenge

Abby admits she used to hate sprint intervals. Like most of her teammates, she groaned when the coach said it was time for intervals. But one day, she was feeling particularly happy and gave a big "WOOT!" and went into the intervals with a big smile. She noticed that they seemed easier. They went by faster, and she was able to give a much harder effort. She asked her coach about it. Her coach said that it's true; when your thoughts are down, your body will be down too. And so began a new tradition of the team whooping it up before intervals.

The high school pool is relatively warm, making getting into easier. However, some of the pools at different schools are much colder, and Luke is not a fan of getting into cold water. Cold water does make for faster swim times, but getting in… BRRRR! He decided to imagine he was a polar bear dunking into the water to cool off. The image of himself wearing a swimsuit over a furry white coat made him laugh so hard he almost choked, but he completely disengaged his mind from the shock of getting into a cold pool.

Cry in Training, Laugh in Competition

> *"If you only ever give 90% in training then you will only ever give 90% when it matters."*
> *~ Michael Owen, soccer player*

Crying in training and laughing in competition doesn't mean you should hate training to the point you cry. The point is to put everything into training and push yourself wayyyy past your "limits." Training should be more demanding than the competition.

Here are some ways to make training much more challenging than competition:

Eat the Frog First

Ewwww! It's a silly saying that comes from deep wisdom. If you eat the frog first, everything else is yummy. If you just do what you're most scared of doing first, before you do anything else, everything else will seem easy. We often spend a lot of mental energy worrying about failing when we try the big thing — a new move, a new tactic, etc. — that we aren't fully present for the easier things. Why not take that load off your shoulders (and get it out of your head!) by just doing the thing you're scared of? DIVE IN! Get it over with! The next time you do it, it'll be easier, and you'll get better at it.

Every time you "eat the frog," you give your self-confidence a HUGE boost.

Train in Chaotic Conditions

Never expect to have the perfect conditions for your training, whether mental or physical. The stars will never be aligned. There will always be homework, exams, scheduling conflicts, and social stuff that gets in the way. Life is messy, and it will never set you up for success. YOU have to do that. Train in conditions your competitors don't train in (yep, rain and sleet, and snow). Learn to focus even if you have an awful earworm.

Train When You Don't Feel Like It

In practice, your coach tells you what to do even if you don't feel like it. But what about your mental training? You won't benefit from mental training if you do it once in a while. You need to be ruthless with yourself and train your mind even if you don't want to. The good thing is that once you automate certain thoughts through enough repetition, it becomes easy and natural.

CHAPTER 6

STRATEGY #3 OF BEING UNSTOPPABLE — GENERATE A POWERFUL ROUTINE

66

"The secret of your future is hidden in your daily routine."

~ Mike Murdock, singer-songwriter

A routine is the foundation for success.

You may have heard that it takes 10,000 hours to master something. Malcolm Gladwell said in *Outliers: The Story of Success*, that breaking this barrier sets winners apart. 10,000 hours is some serious dedication. If you practice for 3 hours a day, that translates to 21 hours a week (weekends included)... 84 hours a week... 336 hours a month... 4,032 hours a year, which leads to nearly 2-½ years of *daily* practice to reach mastery at 10,000 hours.

Of course, few people have the luxury of dedicating their lives to a sport, so expect it to take a lot longer than 2-½ years to master your sport. But the more you can automate some parts of it by creating habits, the faster you progress.

Luke's hero, Michael Phelps, started swimming at 7 years old. By age 10, he had already held a national age group record in the 100-meter butterfly. His coach said that Phelps didn't miss a single day of practice from the ages of 11 to 16. But Phelps didn't stop there. Sundays, birthdays, and even Christmas were training days. When you do the math, at an average four-hour training session in the pool (not even counting gym workouts), Phelps was already well above the 10,000 mark by his Olympic debut in 2000 at 15 years old.

Routine can also be called self-discipline, but from a motivational perspective, the word routine is a more enticing way to get you to create habits that add up to huge results.

Whether you aspire to the highest level in your sport or you just want to have fun as a high school or collegiate athlete, developing a routine will:

- Prevent "analysis paralysis" or wondering what you're supposed to be doing next
- Hold you accountable, especially on days it's tempting to slack off
- Keep you on track to what you want to accomplish
- Measure progress and optimizes performance
- Clearly show you where your weaknesses are
- Allow you to stay in touch with your body and emotions regularly

A routine literally *automates* success because you just do what you gotta do, and rack up "miles" toward your 10,000-hour mastery level.

Your coach has specific sports practice routines that you are expected to adhere to. You can develop routines outside of training to help in all areas of your life.

Most of all, routines are a great way to reduce stress. A bedtime routine can help you destress before bed, so you sleep better. A pre-competition routine helps calm the butterflies. A morning routine puts you in the right mindset for whatever's coming up that day. A study routine makes it easier to keep up with homework and learning.

The Routines of Top Athletes

Whatever their sport, most top athletes swear by a routine. Here are some routines from elite athletes you can adopt as part of every day. Write these down as "Commitments to Myself" or something like that in your workbook.

- Always compete, whether it's in practice or actual competition
- Be careful about what you eat and choose only nutritionally dense foods
- Make sure to get enough sleep every night (according to the American Academy of Sleep

Medicine, children aged 6-12 should regularly sleep 9-12 hours per night and teenagers should sleep 8-10 hours per night)
- Take their recovery seriously
- Set daily goals and track progress on longer-term goals
- Explore other activities to keep their bodies engaged and "guessing"
- Hydrate (being just 2% dehydrated negatively affects strength and endurance); aim for 7-8 glasses of water every day (and more if you're training)
- Practice positive visualization/mental rehearsal (more on this soon)
- Practice empowering self-talk
- Practice having a positive outlook
- Have fun!
- Practice self-discipline
- Practice accepting criticism
- Go easy on social media

Creating a Winning Routine
Everyone has a different training schedule, school demands, jobs, family stuff, etc. so there's no cookie-cutter approach to developing a routine. You can get guidance from an adult you admire or another

young athlete who is particularly dedicated to their sport. Here are the basics:

Time Management

Time management will make your life easier. A schedule should be an organizational tool, not a source of stress. Start with the big picture, break it down into weekly obligations, and then chunk it into a daily plan. Factor in school/homework, family obligations including chores, practice, competition, drive time to/from, and the ever-important downtime.

I recommend, wherever possible, working with your natural rhythms. You know when you feel most awake and alert. That's a great time to schedule homework or practice. The times when you feel less energetic could be devoted to chores, anything that doesn't require a lot of thought, and relaxing.

Create Habits That Support Your Goals

Once you've set a few SMART goals, build habits to support them.

- Homework: Work with your natural rhythms. If you're wide awake after dinner, that's a better time to focus on homework than right after school (if there's no sports practice)
- Snacking: Don't reach for empty calories. Broaden your horizons and eat nutrient-dense snacks like raw nuts, whole fruit, veggies, or dried fruit.
- Sleep: Teens need to prioritize sleep. Avoid scheduling anything that will keep you awake at night. Lack of sleep has been linked to depression and anxiety, not to mention poor athletic performance. As a mom of six, I know how hard mornings can be on everyone if the kids are "underslept" after less than 8-10 hours of sleep! Having a stricter bedtime routine can help ensure you get enough zzz's.
- Downtime: You need it! You deserve it!

Morning Routines

Like most teens, Luke has a hard time waking up early. However, swim practice takes up most of his afternoons, and between that and homework, mornings were the only time he can devote to mental training. His morning routine, which is only about half an hour, goes like this:

- As soon as the alarm rings, Luke gets out of bed. He knows that the snooze button is the button of death that will have him scrambling to get to school on time. It's easier just to get up and get moving. Mel Robbins has a "Five Second Rule": you have five seconds to decide what you will do. It really works!
- He smiles at himself in the mirror, which boosts his mood and confidence. Usually, he'll start to laugh because of his bedhead and sleepy face.
- He drinks a full glass of water to jump-start his metabolism and wake up (try it, it's incredible).
- He stretches and does some yoga to limber up his shoulders, which tend to be tight.
- He does a 5-minute visualization (mental rehearsal) session before showering and getting dressed.
- He has a high-fat and high-protein breakfast to keep him awake in class. His go-to is bacon, eggs,, and a bowl of oatmeal with blueberries.

Abby is a night owl. If she could, she'd be up at the crack of noon and wide awake past midnight. Of course, school schedules don't support that, so she makes sure to get up with plenty of time to drag her sleepy self to school in the morning. Her morning routine goes like this:

- Set the alarm for an hour before the bus comes.
- Set the snooze for 10 minutes.
- Shower (Abby swears a hot shower is the only way to get up) and get dressed; at the same time, she says and sings positive affirmations.
- Dance-up. This is what Abby calls her two-song silly dance to put herself in a happy, energized mood. Yes, it's loud, but her family is very tolerant, and her dad has been known to join in from time to time.
- Journal in Abby's Awesome Life. Most entries revolve around gratitude and self-empowering ideas. (By the way, writing something by hand activates a different part of your brain than typing something, and this helps new ideas stick). This is another reason/purpose for the Workbook.
- Breakfast: According to Abby, bagels are the best thing ever, with a sunny-side-up egg or two.
- Abby lives close to school, so she walks, usually while listening to music and mentally rehearsing a good day in class and on the track.

Toughness Routines

Are there any daily routines that make you tougher? Absolutely.

- A cold shower
- +10 more pushups, squats, etc. beyond your limit
- Admit your mistakes. Own them. Learn from them.
- Wait 15 minutes to eat when you're hungry (delay the gratification).
- Do something you desperately don't want to do for 10 minutes; whether it's difficult, annoying, boring, or embarrassing, *get it out of your head* by just getting it done.
- Sit with your feelings and really feel them, don't push them away with distractions; this is the only way to get them out.

How to Supercharge Any Routine

Whatever your daily routine, there's always room for a small improvement that will yield extraordinary results over time.

Big-picture, you've already set large, medium, and small goals. This section will add jet fuel that will make it easy to adopt positive micro-habits, where the real magic lies in any routine.

"I fear not the man who has practiced 10,000 kicks, but I do fear the man who has practiced one kick 10,000 times." ~ Bruce Lee

Do you think that the guy who practiced one kick 10,000 times has to think about it and talk himself into practicing the kick every day? Probably not. Most likely, he's so used to practicing a kick 50 or 100 times a day that it's as part of his daily life as brushing his teeth. It's *automatic*.

Adding a good habit to your routine is one of the ways to develop mental toughness.

Adopting habits can be hard so to give you a taste of success right away, choose a micro-habit instead. A micro-habit is a habit that takes 1 minute or less to do. The point of micro-habits is that they are ridiculously easy to adopt and easy to add on to over time.

Just One Percent Better

What would things be like if you changed the trajectory of your sport by just one percent? It doesn't seem like much. At first, it's basically the same as what you've been doing. But over time, as the trajectories diverge, the outcomes become noticeable. A tiny change now will mean huge results later.

The British cycling team was known as a losing team for years. Today, they're among the best. They didn't have a dramatic turnaround. The principle they used was improving anything they did — everything that goes into riding a bike — just one percent better, consistently.

A one percent improvement in pedaling efficiency; a one percent improvement in hydration; a one percent improvement in aerodynamics; a one percent improvement in endurance; a one percent improvement in the sprint to the line... right there, you have a five percent improvement, with very little additional effort!

"Habits stay with you even when you don't have the motivation." ~ Neeraj Agnihotri, Author

There is immense power in routine, especially one that incorporates mental mastery. Here's an example of some micro-habits that take less than

ONE MINUTE to do, making them no-brainers to incorporate into your routine:

- 1 minute all-out run
- 1 minute visualizing your ideal game/match/race
- 1 minute balance exercise on your weaker side
- 1 minute strength move on your weaker leg
- 1 minute meditating
- 1 minute repeating a positive affirmation
- 1 minute mentally rehearsing a movement
- 1 minute remembering a success you've had
- 1 minute power pose
- 1 minute smiling at yourself in the mirror (proven to improve confidence and mood)
- 1 minute plank randomly throughout the day

Which of these 10 micro-habits could you adopt today that would help your self-confidence? Write your micro-habit in your Workbook.

There is no struggle to adopt a micro-habit. It's the single most effective way to support major goals. Micro-habits are immune to excuses. They take so little time that it's ridiculous not to do them.

You said this thing was important to you, you said you would do it, and now you are doing it with no excuses.

"Your little choices become habits that affect the bigger decisions you make in life." ~ Elizabeth George

Individually, the significance of the micro-habits that make up your daily routine may seem negligible. But they make your life a little easier. And when you add another micro-habit and another, pretty soon you have the recipe for massive success.

Of that list of sample micro-habits, you might add them up and think, "I can do all of this every day, no problem, because it only takes 10 minutes total. Except, you won't. It's weird; while the brain loves habits, it hates change, and it hates new habits. That's why 1-minute habits are so much easier. Once you do the power pose for 1 minute, add another minute. And another.

Start with one or, at the most, two micro-habits you feel will make the most difference. Don't do anything for more than 1 minute until it's such a part of your daily routine you don't even think about it. Thinking about it defeats the purpose of micro-habits.

Wherever possible, do these habits before starting the rest of your daily routine.

Micro-habits make your daily routine even more effective and efficient in helping you achieve your goals.

Tennis great Serena Williams said, "Do one thing that makes you uncomfortable to help you grow." To Serena's brilliant quote I would add... "And do that one uncomfortable thing until it's your new normal!"

CHAPTER 7

STRATEGY #4 OF BEING UNSTOPPABLE — GROW A WINNER'S MINDSET

"If you can build a muscle, you can build a mindset."

~ Jay Shetty, author

In this chapter, I will show you how to completely rewire your brain for success.

All of us, every single human, have an "operating system" made up of programs instilled in us from birth. They run behind the scenes and determine how we see the world and how we see ourselves. The trouble is, some of these programs are faulty. Nobody is born believing they are unworthy or "less than." These are taught to us, either deliberately or accidentally. So are programs like "You can do anything you set your mind to" and "You can do this!"

Let's circle back to your specific goals. The process of achieving any goal goes like this:

beliefs >>> thoughts >>> feelings >>> actions >>> results

Beliefs

Your beliefs about yourself determine your self-esteem, confidence, and outlook. You must work on developing positive beliefs about yourself. Many athletes believe they are good, but not necessarily "good enough." Disempowering beliefs lead to negative thoughts. Empowering beliefs lead to optimistic thoughts.

Thoughts

Self-limiting beliefs are at the core of poor performance because they lead to negative thoughts. "That team is unbeatable" or "I could never compete at that level" destroy your chances of success because they lead to negative feelings. Think about how you performed when you were feeling anxious or depressed: not great! Negative thoughts lead to negative feelings.

Feelings

What you think dictates how you feel. Your thoughts can generate enthusiasm, fear, joy, doubt, aggression, desire, boldness, frustration, hopelessness, ecstasy, sadness, weakness, etc.

For example, the feeling of shame can greatly impact your ability to perform in a sport.

Negative thoughts lead to feelings that make you hesitate for a hundredth of a second. They lead to feelings of low motivation and hopelessness that make you ease up on training. Negative feelings can lead to giving up.

"Forgive yourself so you can begin to believe you deserve the life you earned." ~ Bianca, Adonis Creed's wife, to Creed, in the film Creed III

Actions

Your choices and actions determine your results, including not taking action because you can't decide what to do.

Results

Your results are the outcomes of your beliefs. What you believe ultimately drives your results.

The good news is that *you can change your beliefs* and develop unshakeable mental toughness to the point you are unstoppable.

Erasing Self-Limiting Beliefs

"What are you looking back for? Look forward." ~ Adonis Creed in the film Creed III

Self-limiting beliefs are negative beliefs about yourself that you've picked up from personal experience, your parents or other adult influences, peers, and society. They make you feel not good enough or unworthy, and they limit what you can achieve.

How to Identify Limiting Beliefs

It's hard to identify your beliefs because they run in the background as part of your "this is how things are" worldview. You can identify them by listening to what you say to and about yourself. See if any of these sound familiar:

- **Age:** *I'm too [young/too old] to [compete at this level/learn this skill]*
- **Personal traits:** *I'm stupid, I'm ugly, I'm clumsy*
- **Feelings:** *I'm too embarrassed to try this [trick, skill] in front of my teammates/friends*
- **Prejudice:** *White men can't jump; Black women aren't*

good swimmers. The belief that your gender, race, sexual orientation, etc., somehow makes you unsuitable for excellence or success in a sport.

- **Disapproval:** Your parents or family doesn't want you to participate in this sport. Usually, you'll hear and adopt things like, "You're too (x) to..." or "You don't have the body for that." With enough repetition, you'll start to believe it and agree with them. *I'm too tall to be a dancer. I don't have the body type to be a sprinter. I'm too short and scrawny to play football.*

- **Missed boat:** *I missed my chance; it's too late, the season's almost over, and I'm already behind.*

- **Time:** *I don't have the time to practice because of school or work*

- **Financial:** *I don't have money to buy the equipment or hire a coach to help me with my biggest challenges.*

- **Perfectionism:** *If I can't be perfect at this, why bother even trying?* If only perfection is acceptable, even the slightest mistake makes you crumble and lose all self-confidence and self-esteem.

Without beating yourself up, identify the *negative* things you say about yourself, your sport, your abilities, how you feel about your chances, your goals, and so forth.

Pay attention to any times you use the word "can't." Pay attention to excuses. Pay attention to rationalizations (or "reasons" you can't do something). Pay attention to how you feel. These are all signs of negative beliefs.

Wherever you feel frustrated, bored, hopeless, angry, jealous, unworthy, incapable, stupid, hesitant, indecisive, etc. Those are often signs of an underlying negative belief, usually tied to "I'm not good enough."

Take the time to write down all of the negative things you say to yourself, whether you actually "believe" them or if they're just what your parents or coaches say all the time. You're about to learn how to undo this programming!

How to Change Limiting Beliefs

All beliefs, whether empowering or limiting, are part of your brain's "operating system." They will continue to run in the background and drive your thoughts, feelings, and actions until they are reprogrammed.

Abby used to struggle with a belief (fueled by some "mean girls" at school) that she was too short to be able to keep up with her long-legged teammates who were a foot taller. They told Abby she had to run twice as fast just to keep up! This affected Abby for a while until one day she learned that tiny hummingbirds can fly at 60 mph. Suddenly she thought of the taller girls as blue herons: graceful for sure, but much slower than the energetic hummingbird!

Change Your Self-Talk

It's important to be aware of the way you talk to and about yourself. You are your best supporter and worst enemy! If your self-talk isn't very nice, learn to talk to yourself as you would talk to your best friend. Encourage, don't judge. Support, don't belittle. Whenever you catch yourself trash-talking yourself, STOP and rephrase what you just said in a positive way.

- Instead of "I really screwed up that free throw" say, "I can see where I made the mistake in my free throw. I'm going to practice making it more fluid."

- Instead of "I am so sick and tired of being benched all the time" say, "I need to sit down with Coach and ask him where I can improve so I get more time on the field."
- Instead of "I'm such a loser for not giving 100% when she was pulling ahead" say, "Okay, well, that happened. Now I know what not to do next time."
- Instead of "I'm not good enough to play varsity" say, "Playing varsity is my goal, and I'm taking steps to make it happen."
- Instead of "I always choke in a big race" say, "I love what I do, this is fun and even though I've had trouble focusing in the past, today I'm just out there to do my best and have fun."

"I need you to let go of your fear. Let go of the guilt. Let go of whatever was and walk into what is." ~ Creed's wife Bianca, from the film Creed III

There's always a way to put a positive and encouraging spin on what you say to yourself. Practice, and you'll make speaking kindly to yourself your new normal.

Keep Moving Forward

You'll also shatter negative beliefs by sticking with your goal-setting strategy no matter how much you doubt yourself. Every small achievement is a hole you poke in a belief that says "you can't do this."

Challenge Your Beliefs

Call yourself out on absolute statements like "always" and "never." They're absurd and wrong! Challenge any beliefs that don't make you feel good!

Whenever you say, "I always choke during an important game" remind yourself that there has been at least *one* game (and who cares if you were just eight years old and it was a backyard game of dodgeball) when you had fun, you *didn't* choke, you had a blast, and you won. The point is, you do not "always" choke.

Practice proving to yourself that any absolute negative belief is absolutely wrong.

Go Back to the Beginning

Think about when and how you acquired certain beliefs about yourself. Was it a nasty thing somebody said to you that you took to heart, like Abby? Was it something drilled into you by a coach or a parent? Was it an experience where you were embarrassed or humiliated?

If you trace a belief back to its origins you might find that it doesn't even apply to you anymore. At the time, you unconsciously adopted that belief and it has stuck... but is it true, and is it relevant?

It's time to get rid of those disempowering beliefs!

The Art of Self-Reprogramming

Positive affirmations, positive self-talk, and visualization (mental rehearsal) are ways to literally reprogram your mind to championship-level mental toughness. The best part is that you are in control: it's like hypnosis in a way except that you are 100% in charge of what ideas you put into your head.

Step 1. Relax

It's important to be in a very relaxed meditative state for new ideas to absorb into your "operating system." This is so that your logical mind doesn't start arguing with you.

To get into a relaxed state, simply close your eyes and breathe deeply for a few minutes. This stimulates your parasympathetic nervous system and your brain activity shifts into what's known as the alpha state. This is the state you're in when you're being super creative: alert, yet very relaxed and focused. Your mind isn't as chatty, you feel happier and calmer, and your mind is much more open to new ideas.

Many people find that self-reprogramming is much easier to do first thing in the morning before your mind starts getting busy thinking about the day.

Step 2: Choose the Right Words

Positive affirmations are one way to reprogram your mind. An affirmation simply confirms "this is what I believe" for better or for worse!

Anything you repeat to yourself over and over again (or for that matter, anything you hear from others over and over or see repeatedly, will "stick" in your mind and create patterns of thought, which then create beliefs.

Inside your mind are billions (or more?) of neural pathways. When you repeat certain thoughts you make these pathways stronger and more efficient, making it easier to think that thought. Your brain loves to automate thoughts. The less work it has to do, the happier it is. Long ago when you were learning to tie your shoes you had to think about every little movement, how to loop the laces, make "bunny ears" and so on. Today you just tie your shoes without thinking about it and your brain is happy because it can be busy with more complex things.

Think about the stories you tell. When you're telling someone about a particularly memorable game or tournament, vacation, or whatever, you get in the habit of telling the same story over and over because it's easier than telling a new story about the same thing every time. The more you repeat a phrase (whether it's empowering or disempowering), the faster and more efficient that pathway becomes.

Just as disempowering thoughts got programmed through repetition, you can create neural highways of positive thoughts.

I'm a huge fan of the voice memo feature on my phone. I have a list of 100s of positive affirmations that I recorded in my own voice, and I pop my headphones in and play them back when I'm out for a walk, cleaning the house, whatever.

"I'm the champ!" ~ Adonis Creed, from the film Creed III

Here are some examples:

- If I can imagine it, I can achieve it.
- If you want this, you can go get it!
- Every day, in every way, I'm getting better and better.
- You have come so far! Keep pushing!
- I can do this!
- You got this!
- I am calm and focused.
- You are in the Zone.
- I wanted to do this and I'm doing it!
- You're strong, fast, brave, and tough!
- It's not easy but I can do it!

- Go have fun!
- I am unstoppable!

When you make up your own affirmations, the rules are:

- Use both "I" and "you" statements (because we believe what others say about us more than we believe what we say about ourselves)
- Use the present tense: "I am," "You have," etc.
- Avoid using any negative words like "don't" because your brain doesn't register them: for example, "I won't skip practice" focuses on the negative and all your brain hears is "skip practice." Instead, rewrite the statement to focus on what you want, like "I get stronger in practice."

Ready for the "secret sauce"?

Step 3: Add Emotion

Mindlessly mumbling affirmations won't do anything. You have to attach emotion to them. Emotions are what make words stick, for better or worse.

When you say or record your affirmations, say them with a huge smile on your face. Say them as if you were saying them to your best friend. Say them with enthusiasm. Energy. Power. Self-love.

Step 4: Visualize

Worrying uses your imagination to visualize the worst possible outcome. You can also choose to visualize the best possible outcome. This is not easy at first but like anything it gets easier with practice.

Imagine yourself having achieved your goal. How do you feel in that moment? Who's around you? What are you wearing? What song is playing? Where are you? Engage your senses in this daydream. Make it real in your mind.

When you visualize, make sure you don't see yourself, but that you see things from your perspective.

Step 5: Repeat

Some of the affirmations/new beliefs you want to imprint in your brain will come easily. Others, not so much. Use repetition and emotion. Just as you practice the same physical moves over and over, practice these mental moves over and over *until you believe them.* This could take weeks or several months. Stick with it just like you stick with your training.

Remember that every win you have, every challenge you overcome, and every milestone you achieve will support your belief that YOU CAN.

Managing Social Media

We've discussed how what you repeatedly see and hear programs your mind in a certain way. We talk about how coaches, teachers, and parents influence beliefs; but what about social media influencers? You guessed it: social media can be a wonderful source of inspiration or it can completely erode your self-esteem.

The Good

Social media has changed the world and a lot of good has come from it.

- It's a great way to connect to people from all over the world including other athletes and fans.
- It's a surprisingly awesome source of free and highly engaging knowledge and content. As an athlete, you can find a lot of free tips on technique, training, inspiration, and motivation.

- It's good for your daily dose of laughter.

The Bad

Studies are showing that excessive social media activity is bad for you.

- Endless scrolling is addictive because the algorithm ensures that you get repeated dopamine hits and who doesn't love your brain's own happy drug?
- It can negatively affect mental health and contribute to feelings of isolation and loneliness when you compare yourself to people on social media.
- It contributes to information overload and overwhelm, which can cause anxiety and depression if the information in your feed skews toward the negative.
- It doesn't contribute to (and may erode) the development of interpersonal skills such as eye contact and undivided attention.
- Cyberbullying can make you feel terrible about yourself and promotes a hate culture.
- Late-night scrolling disrupts sleep.
- It invades your privacy.
- It can distract you from your goals and cause you

to procrastinate.

- It shortens your attention span and promotes loss of concentration. *When your mind becomes accustomed to short clips, you lose the ability to sustain focus for longer periods putting an athlete at a huge disadvantage.*

Star athletes are very much in the public eye on social media. On the plus side, it lets them form relationships with their fans. But, it can be a burden too. Sponsored athletes need to have a social media presence to promote their sponsors. No one is immune to trolls and the truly ugly, hateful, hurtful, and hostile comments that they make.

Does this mean you have to completely abstain from social media? It doesn't have to be all or nothing. First, limit your scrolling time. This falls under the first tenet of mental toughness: commitment. Which is most important to you, your sport, or social media?

Luke maintains several social media accounts but has made a commitment to stop the scroll after 15 minutes. He sets a timer and most of the time, admittedly not 100% of the time, he puts the phone down and starts his homework. He tries to avoid using his phone around bedtime because of the blue light emissions that interfere with sleep. Luke uses social media for inspiration, and to share the realities of his training and competition with his followers. He considers his followers as his team. He can't make it without them, and sharing his experiences makes them feel like they're part of his success.

Abby is extremely careful with what appears in her feed. She doesn't follow pop celebrities, only athletes. She doesn't react to any stories that make her stressed or unhappy. She blocks anyone who spews negativity and hate. She actively interacts with profiles that share knowledge or anything inspirational. She practices the age-old wisdom, "If you have nothing nice to say, don't say anything" and calls out bullies. Abby takes inspiration from people she admires... With caution. She knows that reality is very different from the idealized clips on her feed. Abby limits her social media to 10 minutes a day. She's the first to admit this is hard. But she's very proud of her ability to stick to this short indulgence.

How to Avoid Social Media Addiction

With social media being such a part of everyone's lives, the key to preventing becoming addicted to it is self-control.

Set a Timer

It takes discipline to stop the scroll. Setting a timer and sticking to it is a commitment to yourself, especially at night. Check out your phone settings. Many phones have a screen time downtime setting to help you prioritize feeling good in the morning over a late night of entertainment.

Change Your Perspective

Social media algorithms keep showing you content they think you will like for the simple purpose of keeping you engaged so they can show you more advertisements. When you look at social media as one big commercial with a little bit of content thrown in, you might lose your taste for it.

Actively Look For the Good

Seek out knowledge and inspiration from athletes or anyone who posts motivational content that resonates with you. They're a good resource whenever you need a pick-me-up!

Don't hesitate to unfollow or block anyone that posts negative, depressing, overly dramatic click-bait content.

Think of your social media as part of your team. Seek out and interact with those that have a friendly and supportive team spirit. Everyone else doesn't need to be part of your life.

Be Kind

Think before you post, react, or respond.

Don't Let the Negativity In

There will always be haters and people who just don't bother to consider the consequences of their comments. Don't let the negative comments get in your head and affect your outlook and performance. Don't take it personally because what people say is 100% a reflection of who they are and it has nothing to do with you.

The Takeaway

This chapter is hefty. It can be a lot to take in all at once! If you take just one thing from this chapter, let it be this: Be very aware of what you consume, and

I'm not just talking about food.

The words you hear and the things you see all contribute to your inner programming. By surrounding yourself with positive, inspiring, empowering, and supportive people and using the self-reprogramming steps I've outlined, you can change any negative programming and become unstoppable.

Your Chance To Hit A Ball For The Future Of Our Young Champions of Tomorrow!
"It ain't over 'til it's over." — Yogi Berra

At the start of the book, we talked about the importance of a Champion's Mindset, then the Science behind Mental Toughness, and shared some inspiring stories. The 7 Proven Strategies of Becoming Unstoppable are KEY to your success on and off the field. The driving force behind this book is to motivate and inspire you with actual strategies to build your mental toughness in any sport.

If we're doing it right, we can learn from the mistakes of our past... and if we're really paying attention, we can learn from the mistakes of others too.

But mistakes aren't our only guiding force. We learn through studying, watching, practicing, and sharing our experiences. This is where you, as the reader, have a chance to be part of the teaching process for the champions of tomorrow.

After all, this is what many of the biggest MLB stars do. Take Cal Ripken Jr., who, along with his brother, founded the Cal Ripken Sr. Foundation. This foundation helps establish softball and baseball programs for at-risk youth and works to create playing fields and youth development parks.

Stars like Ripken take their experiences and everything they've learned throughout their careers to help the next generation follow in their footsteps.

You may need more resources or career experience from Ripken, but you do have an opportunity to contribute to helping other players up their game.

By leaving a review of this book on Amazon, you'll show other young athletes who want to improve their mental toughness where they can find the guidance they're looking for.

Remember to grab the Workbook that compliments this book!!!

Simply by telling other readers how this book helped you and what they can expect to find inside, you'll set them on the road to improving their mental toughness and game.

Thank you for your support. Sharing our knowledge and experiences helps nurture great talent and keep the game alive.

Scan the QR CODE below to LEAVE A FAVORABLE REVIEW.

THANK YOU!!!

CHAPTER 8

STRATEGY #5 OF BEING UNSTOPPABLE — ESTABLISH SELF-MASTERY

"**Be like a duck. Calm on the surface, but always paddling like the dickens underneath.**"

~ Michael Caine, actor

In this chapter, you will learn to manage pre-competition nerves and stay calm under pressure before and during the event. Pre-competition anxiety is part of sports. All athletes experience it to one degree or another. Some simply manage it better than others.

Michael Phelps was famous for his pre-competition anxiety. He might have looked calm and composed on the outside, but he has admitted that he struggled with severe anxiety and depression. His advice? Get help. Talk to someone you trust, someone supportive and positive.

Know Your Triggers

Are you aware of what triggers your anxiety? Anxiety triggers can include:

Lack of Experience

Less seasoned competitive athletes often have more trouble managing being pumped up for competition. Learn to view the situation as exciting rather than intimidating.

Abby likes to treat every competition as "practice, but with prizes."

Fear of Repeating the Past

You may feel anxious about repeating a past failure or suffering yet another serious injury. Staying in the moment and treating this situation as a completely fresh blank slate can help.

Problems with Fitness, Form, or Technique

These fears arise when you feel unprepared. Mental rehearsal can help significantly, both during training and pre-event.

Also, keep in mind that your coach would not let you compete if you were horribly unprepared.

If you're coming back from an injury and your coach believes you have the form it takes to compete, *adopt that point of view!*

If you're struggling with a technique or move and yet your coach is asking you to compete, it's probably because the experience will do you good whatever the outcome. *Adopt that point of view!*

Lack of Team Support

Individual-sport athletes are more prone to anxiety than team-sport athletes because teammates help talk each other off the cliff in clutch situations. In a solo competition, the spotlight is on you. There's no one to cheer in victory, no one to blame in defeat. *Expect to do your best and have fun. Period.*

You can get over feeling out there all alone by making friends with your competitors. You're in this together! You're here to have fun and do your best and it's a show of sportsmanship to support each other because *that* helps bring out the best in an individual whether you're on the giving or receiving side of emotional support.

Lack of Family/Fan Support

Away games/events mean a small fan base for emotional support. Ask family and friends to come to support you and if they can't, a quick video chat with someone supportive before the competition can help.

Personal Issues

Family problems, financial troubles, poor grades, competition for college acceptance, exam pressures, breaking up with a boyfriend/girlfriend, or the loss of a loved one can all make you lose focus and take the joy out of competition. You could think of sports as a way to "burn off" some of the stress and strong feelings that surround personal issues.

High Expectations/Pressure to Perform

Expectations lead to anxiety whether it's coming from school/coach/peers/parents, but mostly your own expectations. The expectations of helicopter parents are awful but an athlete's own expectations are often even worse. You don't want to disappoint anyone. You don't want to disappoint yourself. You don't want to look bad when you make a mistake. You don't want to be seen as a loser.

Remember, no matter the situation, you can't do anything except your best, and you can't control the rest. *Expect nothing except doing your best and having fun. Period.*

Uncertainty

The outcome isn't certain even if you're a world record holder. Things happen that you can't control, but you can always control your reaction. *Nothing in life is guaranteed, not even your next breath. You might as well relax and have fun.*

The Significance of the Event

The bigger the event, the bigger the stress. Try to look at it from this point of view: What one athlete sees as pressure another athlete sees as a fun challenge. *You've done this hundreds of times in training. You've competed before. You can do it now.*

One of the best tactics I've ever heard for managing competition stress is to just decide to have more fun than your competitors.

Fear of Ridicule, Embarrassment, or Letting Others Down

When you want so badly to win and you are afraid you won't, this affects your performance.

When you fear being ridiculed or embarrassed because of a loss, this also makes you choke. The same goes for fears of letting your coach, team, or school down. Nobody should be under that kind of pressure but as long as you give your best, people will appreciate the effort regardless of the outcome.

Is it Jitters or Anxiety?

Every competition is different. You might find yourself mildly excited at some, and freaking out at others. Check-in with yourself whether you're just feeling pre-competition excitement or actual anxiety.

Pre-Competition Jitters

Pre-competition jitters or "butterflies" are a sign that your body has dumped a lot of adrenaline and other hormones into your bloodstream in preparation for action. That's a good thing! You may feel excitement ("I can't wait for this race/game to start!"); highly alert; clarity of thought; rapid heart rate and nervous energy like a tightly wound spring. The biggest difference is that soon after the event or race starts, you settle into it and start to have fun. In other words, you're ready to play.

Pre-Competition Anxiety

You feel the same symptoms as if you have the jitters, but instead of clarity of thought, your mind keeps going toward the worst possible imagined scenario. This may result in physical symptoms like muscle weakness or stiffness, excessive sweating, shaking, queasiness, or heart palpitations. Emotionally you may feel feelings of dread or fear. You may be irritable or aggressive, and you may have a strong desire for a way out of the competition.

How to Manage Anxiety

"I don't think you're human if you don't get nervous," said Sidney Crosby, two-time Olympic gold medalist, World and Junior World champion, two-time National Hockey League Most Valuable

Player, three-time Stanley Cup Champion, and six-time National Hockey League all-star.

However, anxiety manifests in you, having people tell you to relax doesn't help because they don't know what's going on in your head!

Anxiety is part of competitive sports at any level and it doesn't look the same for everyone. You might feel fear, increased heart rate, indecision, a dry mouth, sweaty palms, a knot in your stomach, trembling, a desire to run away, stony silence, muscle tension, nausea, inability to concentrate, digestive problems, avoidance behaviors like nail biting or avoiding eye contact, excess chattiness, weakness, and lots of negative self-talk and negative visualization (worry).

I recommend you read through this section and choose one technique that you feel you can use in your next competition. Pick just one technique so you're not overwhelmed. Once you master that technique, add another, and so on, Take it slow and master as many of these as you can.

Acknowledge Your Feelings

It's okay to acknowledge that you feel anxious! The best of the best of the best have puked at the starting line! Don't try to push the anxiety away and ignore it because it won't be ignored. Sometimes just acknowledging that you feel anxious is enough to cool things down.

It's just your brain doing its very best to keep you safe both physically and emotionally. You can thank your brain for working hard to keep you from doing something that could hurt you. I know it sounds silly, but simply acknowledging that your brain is just trying to help can tone down the anxiety. Tell yourself, "I've done this before and I was just fine. Let's go out there and have fun!"

And it's important to RELEASE those emotions. Let them out. Bottling up emotions does not do you any good. Cry if you feel like it, until there's not a single tear left. And I know, sitting there in front of your teammates and coaches and the entire world, you want to look strong. Excuse yourself and cry it out in private. Cry until there's no more crying in you, then take a deep breath and go out there and crush it.

Stand Like a Champion

You know how people stand on the podium: legs slightly apart, hands in the air, chest out, chin up, a big smile on their faces... Believe it or not, this stance (which is a lot like Leonardo da Vinci's "Vitruvian Man" actually increases testosterone production if you hold it for about 2 minutes! For real! It's called the power pose. Don't worry, ladies, you're not going to grow hair on your chest, it's a very small testosterone boost that will increase your physical energy, focus, and confidence! Do it in the locker room, or even a bathroom stall if you don't want people to see you... Or do it as a team right on the field. Hold that pose for 2 minutes. Feel the power! ROAR if you want to!

Listen to Music

Use music to calm or energize you, whatever you need at the moment. I'm not going to tell you what kind of music to listen to. You know what makes you feel good and happy. Abby's go-to is bluegrass. Luke likes techno.

Breathe Deeply

Breathing exercises that focus on the physical experience of deep, slow breathing can help calm your nervous system and take your mind off your stress. Here are two breathwork exercises to try:

Close your eyes, and put one hand on your abdomen. Breathe in deeply and slowly through your nose. Feel your abdomen rise. Hold your breath for a moment, then exhale as much of the air in your lungs through your mouth as you can. Repeat 10x. Not only does this calm your body, but it also helps release any carbon dioxide in your lungs that you've been holding on to because of shallow and anxious breathing. This will oxygenate your muscles and you might even perform better than anticipated.

The box breath that Navy SEALS use calms your nervous system and helps your body release stress: inhale for 4, hold for 4, exhale for 4, hold for 4. You can do this to the rhythm of walking or just count it out.

"Listen!"

When your mind gets stuck in a worry loop and you can't shut it up, command it to stop by saying, "Listen!" For a few moments, your mind will go absolutely quiet, because it doesn't know what it's supposed to listen for. And you'll experience blissful mental silence. This is a great way to break a mental worry loop. Repeat as needed. You can also use other commands like "Not now" or "It's okay!" to break the loop.

Mentally Rehearse Ease

"The less effort, the faster and more powerful you will be."
~ Bruce Lee, martial artist/actor

The more you practice something the better you do it to the point where even difficult moves flow easily. Take this to a new level by mentally rehearsing ease. When your body and mind are working together perfectly, the movements can be physically incredibly demanding, and yet there's a sense of ease. This is the Flow state, or being "in the Zone."

Luke likes to visualize the smoothest, most fluid butterfly stroke possible. He imagines his opponents flailing around in the water, splashing and kicking their way across the pool, while he is as smooth as a dolphin, making barely a ripple on the water as he glides effortlessly in front of the other swimmers. He visualizes this effortless stroke taking him all the way across the pool, lap after lap, to victory.

Have More Fun

Tell yourself to go out there and have more fun than your competition. Let them be stressed and tense! You do you and have fun. If you're out there to have fun playing your sport, you'll be more relaxed. Athletes with smiles on their faces usually perform better!

Mentally Rehearse Every Possible Scenario, Even the Ridiculous Ones

Michael Phelps was famous for being a master at mental rehearsal. Phelps said that he mentally rehearsed every conceivable scenario. Whatever could possibly happen, from a perfect record-breaking swim to a leg cramp, ripped suit, or broken goggles, he already knew exactly what he would do. Nothing caught Phelps off guard. This exercise gave him a calm confidence that he carried into every race.

Stop projecting what could happen if you make a mistake or lose. Give equal time to potential positive outcomes! Once in competition, you can relax and be in the moment knowing that you have mentally prepared for any scenario. You have Plans A, B, and all the way through Z. You're ready.

Repeat a Mantra

Abby is a big fan of mantras. Ever since she adopted Yoda's "Try not. Do, or do not. There is no try!" as a mantra for when she's feeling unsure of herself, she has come up with several others that help ease her mind before competition. "I have had a great race before, and I can have one right now" is one of her favorites.

Luke likes to ask himself, "What's important now?" when he starts feeling anxious. The WIN ("what's important now"?) strategy helps him stay focused on what he can do right now, instead of worrying about the future. Write your W.I.N in your Workbook.

Create a Pre-Competition Ritual

Most athletes have a pre-competition ritual. Michael Jordan, one of the all-time greatest basketball players, had a special free throw ritual that would help calm his body and focus his attention. He would spin the basketball in his hands, then bounce it exactly three times, spin it once more while looking at the rim of the hoop, and then take the shot.

Have you ever watched downhill skiers visualize the course, sitting in the snow with their eyes closed, leaning into the turns, "tucking" before a jump, and knocking gates out of the way... And then they open their hand, and you see their good luck charm, which they kiss before tucking it into their skinsuit? Partly, they are using this valuable pre-race time to mentally rehearse their run, and partly, they are self-soothing with a personal ritual.

Some athletes meditate. Some shake their bodies to release muscle tension. Some have their headphones on, jamming to their favorite soundtrack while they warm up. Some kiss their good luck charm. Some pray.

Some people need to psych themselves up and build energy. Some need to release energy and calm down. Create a ritual for yourself. Do whatever works for *you*.

The **5-Senses Check-In** can help you bring your focus back to the moment. Name:

- One thing you taste: dry mouth, an energy gel, water, electrolyte drink, gum, etc. (identifying what you're tasting right now is hard when you're not actually eating, and it's a powerful way to bring focus to the moment)
- Two things you smell: gym bag, fresh grass, a leather ball, pool water, etc.
- Three things you hear: whistles, the crowd cheering, people talking, music, etc.
- Four things you can touch: body, equipment, ground, mat, water, racquet, ball, etc.
- Five things you can see: this one is the easiest and often the most distracting, so focus on seeing five things related to your W I N

Trust Your Training

Trust your training to put yourself in the right mindset. Confidence in your abilities comes from feeling that you have done everything you can to prepare for competition. If you feel good about how hard you've worked in preparation for the event, you'll feel more confident.

Two-time NBA MVP Stephen Curry relies on taking more than 2,000 shots every week (250+ every day, plus 100 more before a game).

Focus on What You Can Control

There are aspects of the competition that are out of your control. You can control one thing: YOU. Practice controlling your breathing. Practice controlling where your eyes go. Practice controlling the way you walk. Practice taking a deep breath and holding it. Practice shaking the tension out of your body. Practice ignoring negative thoughts. Practice giving pep talks to your teammates. Practice holding a smile until you can't help but crack up.

Turn Past Failures Into Strength

If past failures are coming back to haunt you, remind yourself how far you've come since then. Even if it was just yesterday! You have probably gone over the event a bazillion times, analyzing every nuance of every moment... Well, guess what? Now you know what not to do. That's why failures are so important in sports!

Relive Your Past Achievements

You can draw energy from thinking about your past successes in your sport and in other areas. If you succeeded before, you can succeed now. It doesn't matter if it was a big win or a tiny win! A win is a win. Let it fuel you.

Remember, achieving your past goals is a win. Even if you're looking at the tiniest of goals, you won because you achieved them. Every time you learn from a mistake or failure, it's a win because you won't do "that" next time.

Most of all, reliving your past achievements shows that you have a history of achieving. A history of winning.

Be Grateful

Cultivate an attitude of gratitude. How awesome that you have the opportunity and the privilege to compete in your sport! How amazing that you've come so far from when you were a beginner! You've worked hard to get here so be thankful for the opportunity to do what you love.

Turn Fear Into Excitement

There's a fine line between anxiety and excitement: both are highly aroused states with very similar physiological elements.

Think about a time when you were very excited about something. Tune into that energy. How does excitement show up in your body? What do you feel, and how intense is it?

Now think about a time when you were very anxious about something. Tune into that energy. How does anxiety show up in your body? What do you feel, and how intense is it?

Get excited about having fun. No fear, just fun.

Detach From the Outcome

You can't tell yourself not to feel something but you *can* practice detaching from the outcome. If you feel excited and happy about *participating* in a game or event, that puts you in a different mindset than if you expect that you might lose. So what if everyone's all dressed up in their team uniforms and the bleachers are full? Decide to go out there and have *fun*.

I just got home from College Dance Nationals in Florida. One of the teams wanted to win soooo bad. They trained one dance into the ground with 3x/ day practices. They did not diversify by having two routines. Apparently, some girls were crying right before going into prelims because they were that scared and had so much pressure. For a moment, they lost the joy of dance and being there. Just like the story of the Olympic athlete who trained so hard and put so much pressure on himself for his last Olympics that he wasn't winning. Then in his last couple of events, he literally said to himself, "What the hell. This is my last time competing. I'm gonna enjoy it. For the love of the sport." Then went out and not only won gold but crushed it, beating all previous times.

There's a lot of pressure to win, but that pressure can cause you to choke. Tell yourself that you are committed to *doing your best and having fun no matter the outcome*. Then, win or lose, you can feel good about yourself.

You are only anxious when you are attached to an outcome, and you don't want to be disappointed if it doesn't work out. Expect to simply do your best and have fun — and watch most of your anxiety melt away! Let go of any *attachment* to winning. I know this is hard, and it takes a lot of practice, but it's truly a game-changer.

OK: you're prepared for the big event. What do you do if things go sideways during competition? That's next!

How To Avoid Choking During Competition

In 2001, cricketer Scott Boswell had The Day From Hell when he choked during the finals. His anxiety was so bad that he froze. Years and years of training and competition, and now he couldn't do something that he had done hundreds of times before? Three weeks before the final, he wasn't sure if he was even going to be selected for the finals. His coach asked Scott whether he was up for it — and a seed of doubt was planted. Just 45 minutes before the game, Scott got word that he was in. At first, everything was going fine. But then, he made a mistake. The ball didn't come out of his hand the way it should. He bowled again and made another mistake and then another and another.

Nothing was going right, it's as if he had never held a ball in his hand. The crowd took notice, and things went from bad to worse. The louder the crowd got, the more Boswell started rushing and each bowl was worse than the last. He said, "Unfortunately, I sped things up when pressure got to me, rather than trying to slow it down and take a step back, do the breathing, have a little smile – 'It's only a game of cricket, off you go.'"

Boswell found himself stuck in overthinking, frantically thinking about how to execute skills that normally came naturally and automatically. His specialty was suddenly foreign to him. He felt absolutely incompetent. He said, "When your conscious mind doesn't trust your subconscious mind, you've got an issue. When you're in the flow, and you're not thinking about it, you just bowl, and you just trust your skills. [That day] I just didn't trust myself. I didn't trust my action and I didn't trust my skill set, and then when it was put under high pressure, it failed." This day would live in eternal infamy on YouTube.

Sometimes, things don't go as planned during competition. Maybe external circumstances like weather or poor playing conditions make it hard to focus, or you have to play in front of a hostile crowd.

Here's what to do so that you can stay in the game, stay focused, and have fun.

Be Prepared

Knowing that there is exactly ONE thing you have to worry about in any competition — you — means you don't have to waste mental energy worrying. You can't control anything else. If you come physically and mentally prepared, you expect the unexpected. When your mind is in the game, then whatever the situation and the outcome, you can still walk away satisfied knowing you did your best.

Australian Susie Maroney was just 15 when she broke the speed record for swimming across the English Channel in 1990. Okay: that's a huge accomplishment. But did you know she was born with cerebral palsy? And that she didn't finish high school? (Don't get any ideas!) Susie started swimming at four. By seven, she was competing and fell in love with distance swimming at 13. Just two years later she smashed the Channel crossing record. Swimming the cold, treacherous waters of the English Channel doesn't happen without a lot of preparation. Whether you're preparing to swim the English Channel or you're a wide receiver running a fumbled ball almost the entire length of the football field, you've got to be prepared to do your job, no matter what.

Be Here Now

Be in the moment. 100% here, now. Don't think about the big picture or beyond your next move. Ask yourself, "What's my job right now?"

Your objective *right now* is not to win the game, but to take the shot or block the shot. Your objective *right now* is not to stand on the podium but to swim these four laps or perform this routine.

THIS is the most important shot. THIS is the most important hurdle. THIS is the most important flip turn. THIS is the most important vault. You can't change what happened before and if your attention is on what "might" happen your body and mind cannot work as one. Only the present moment matters!

Slow Down

Rushing leads to mistakes and bad decisions. Great quarterbacks are the perfect example of not rushing. You can always tell when a QB is feeling pressured and throws the ball in desperation. Usually, it's a bad throw. But the great QBs wait until the perfect moment to throw, even if there's a wall of linebackers just seconds away from slamming into them.

Stick to the way you've always done it in training. Trust your training. Maintain your routine no matter the pressure.

Laugh About It

Sometimes, absurd things happen. You choose how to react to the unexpected. Let's say your shorts rip in mid-play. You could let that make you self-conscious which will make you lose focus, or you can laugh about it and keep doing your job.

The Takeaway

Looking back at my athletic career, I remember so many times feeling absolutely freaked out to the point of wanting to throw up. Over time, it got easier to manage my emotions. If you're someone who is more easily triggered, then this chapter will give you the self-mastery you need to focus your energy and talents on the competition.

For all of us, the main takeaway is: do your best and have fun!

CHAPTER 9

STRATEGY #6 OF BEING UNSTOPPABLE — MAKE THE MOST OF INJURIES AND FATIGUE

"You should never view your challenges as a disadvantage. Instead, it's important for you to understand that your experience facing and overcoming adversity is actually one of your biggest advantages."

~ Michelle Obama, former First Lady of the United States

When he was eight, Glenn Cunningham nearly lost his legs after a tragic fire that killed his brother Floyd. Because of the severe burns, doctors recommended amputating Cunningham's legs. "Even though the doctor said I'd never walk, he couldn't convince me because I knew I was going to be able to walk again." He eventually recovered but it was a whole year before the boy could walk. Running became an act of defiance. By age 12, Cuningham showed his talent as a runner, even with horribly scarred legs. He competed in the 1932 Olympics and four years later, set the world record for the 800m run. Ultimately the boy who was nearly crippled went on to hold several world records because he defied the odds and said that he would walk again.

Injuries

All athletes will suffer from an injury at some point in their career. Sports injuries can involve the bones, muscles, and connective tissue like tendons, ligaments, and cartilage.

As an athlete, you're already more prone to injury, but then again, you won't die of boredom like you would sitting in a padded chair!

Coping with injury is a mental game of overcoming strong feelings about being unable to participate in your sport. I get it! It's so hard to watch from the sidelines when all you want is to be out there! The best things you can do while injured are:

Sleep

Getting plenty of sleep will give your body time to do its repair work. When you're in deep non-REM sleep, your body produces human growth hormone, or HGH, which is essential for muscle repair and growth. Your body also produces prolactin (a hormone that regulates inflammation) during non-REM sleep.

Food is Medicine

Anti-inflammatory spices like turmeric, protein, and lots of leafy green vegetables will support your body in the healing process.

Medical Advice

It's hard to keep an athlete down, partly because we're used to being in some pain much of the time.

I like to think of it this way: sports should cause temporary muscle pain, which you can sometimes heal with rest and sometimes with active recovery. However, don't be too quick to get back out there when you suffer from "structural pain" from a strained muscle, torn ligament, pulled tendon, or broken bone. Getting back into action too soon will cause long-term damage. Follow your doctor's and/ or physical therapist's guidance: they're not trying to keep you down. They're trying to make sure you heal properly.

Gentle Movement

When you're allowed, gentle movements like walking, cycling, or slow swimming will stimulate the lymphatic system, removing waste from your cells and speeding up healing. It will also keep you from getting stiff and losing all of your fitness.

Mental Rehearsal

Take this time to mentally rehearse whatever aspects of the sport you're struggling with, specific movements, ease, feeling great doing your sport, and winning.

Can you prevent injury? Probably not all injuries, but there's a lot you can do to minimize the chances.

- Wear appropriate protective gear
- Warm up to prime your body for action and cool down to prevent delayed-onset muscle soreness (DOMS)
- Play a variety of sports to avoid always putting stress on the same muscles and joints
- Take rest seriously. Plan for an offseason where you do something completely different than your usual sport
- Eat a healthy diet
- Hydrate to avoid heat-related illness
- Pay attention to form and technique: work with a sports therapist or physical therapist to make sure your form is mechanically correct (for example, no knock-need position on the bike or not having your arms go *back* far enough in a sprint)
- Don't let small injuries go ignored. Compensating for injuries can lead to changes in the way you move, which can cause even more serious injuries. Talk to your coach if you are injured and find ways to maintain your fitness without aggravating the injury.

Fatigue

Most athletes are familiar with fatigue and pushing through it during training or competition. Hydration and fuel will keep you energized, but don't forget what goes on in the background: school pressure, lack of sleep, not enough recovery time, and overtraining will affect how you feel day to day.

Fatigue is just as mental as it is physical.

When an effort feels much harder than it should be, it's easy to lose sight of the "carrot" that motivates you. You just don't care if you get the carrot anymore because the *perceived* effort is harder than it really is. That's when you say, "I can't do it" (even though you've done it a hundred times before), you lose focus and stop making an effort. If that has happened to you, then you were *mentally* fatigued.

The mind will quit long before your body does, but you can train yourself to push past mental fatigue.

Assuming you're taking great care of your body, getting past the, "I can't do it" barrier is part of what makes you mentally tough. Training yourself to stay "in the game" mentally, no matter how you feel physically, can be the difference between winning or losing by a hundredth of a second.

There are several neurotransmitters in the brain that make you feel like "I CAN do it" even if your muscles and lungs are burning and you think you can't take another step:

- Dopamine (reward)
- Endorphins (the body's natural pain killer)
- Acetylcholine (alertness)

Increase dopamine, endorphins, and acetylcholine by reminding yourself of your **Why**. When you *want* that carrot so badly you can taste it, you'll excite the parts of your brain that expect a reward (the carrot), and this will motivate you to greater effort. Even a few seconds of intensely visualizing your Why during a hard effort can be enough to light your inner fire.

It's important to talk to your coach about feeling overtrained and talk to your coach, parents, and teachers about chronic mental fatigue that might come from having too much on your plate.

Abby has one bit of advice about overtraining: don't. When she discovered she was "pretty good" (her words) at running, she wanted more. She wanted to run faster, whatever it took. Another mile? Sure! Skip the day off? Definitely! Eventually, Abby noticed that the more she trained, the slower she got! After a heart-to-heart with her coach, she learned about the value of recovery. Today, she does what many professional athletes do on their days off: nothing! She fights the urge to do a couple of squats (by a couple, she means at least 50) and lets her body chill.

Luke also struggled with the "more is better" mindset, and he would always do more than what his coach wanted: extra laps, extra sprints, and even extra runs on non-swimming days. A shoulder injury forced him to take it easy for a couple of months. The months of recovery led him to realize that his energy was through the roof and he was sleeping better at night. From that experience, Luke vowed to stick to the plan!

In the next chapter, I'm going to give you a cheat sheet for supporting your body with nutrition.

CHAPTER 10

STRATEGY #7 OF BEING UNSTOPPABLE — TAKE CARE OF YOUR BODY

66

"An empty lantern provides no light. Self-care is the fuel that allows your light to shine brightly."

~ Unknown

Alysia Montaño, a seven-time U.S. track and field champion, thinks of her body as an elite sports car that deserves premium fuel. She refuses to put anything but the best in her body so that her food works for her, not against her. She says, "I eat food, and I eat real food." When she can, she chooses unprocessed food but will also occasionally enjoy a pizza or a hot dog.

Garbage In, Garbage Out

What you eat *on a regular basis* has a direct correlation to how you perform in your sport. Once in a while, there's no problem with a bag of Doritos, but don't make them your go-to if you want to enhance physical performance.

You need to educate yourself on nutrition if you're going to excel in your sport, and that's what this chapter is all about. As a high school athlete, your body is still growing, and you're going through a lot of hormonal changes.

The biggest takeaway from this chapter is that nutrition is not one-size-fits-all.

Eating Right For YOU

Just as training needs are different for everyone, so is nutrition. Finding the right balance of nutrient-rich and energy-rich food that supports the demands of your sport is different for everyone, depending on body composition, gender, sport, and age.

Please note, what you're about to read is for your information only, based on the latest research. This section is not intended to be a hard-and-fast dietary guide. Talk to your coach and your doctor about what you should be eating.

Body Composition

There are three basic body types which I'll go over in a moment. One theory suggests that when you eat for your body type (the "body type diet") works with your metabolism, or how well your body processes the nutrients you take in. The reasoning for this is that every body type has unique characteristics in the way that it grows muscle and stores fat and that eating for that particular body type can help you perform better at your sport.

Main Body Types and Hybrids

Ectomorph: thin, lanky, with smaller bone structure and shoulders that are narrower than the hips. May have trouble gaining weight and have a hard time developing a more muscled physique. Many ectomorphs are endurance athletes.

Ecto-Mesomorph: lean and muscular, athletic-looking. Has more trouble gaining weight than mesomorphs and endomorphs.

Mesomorph: medium frame with athletic musculature. Girls will be developing an hourglass figure, and both genders have shoulders broader than their hips. Find it easy to gain or lose weight and find it easy to build muscle. May excel in sports that require quick bursts of speed and power or "all-around" sports that require a combination of speed, agility, power, and endurance.

Meso-Endomorph: strong, but without a "chiseled" look (football players are an example)

Endomorph: large bone structure, larger hips and midsection. Boys in this category are labeled stocky and girls are labeled curvy. Tend to carry more body fat than the other groups and may have trouble losing it, but endomorphs are also more muscular, and this body type excels at power sports.

Please do not let body type groupings discourage you from playing a sport that doesn't appear to fit your body type!!

There may be "ideal" body types for all sports, but that doesn't mean outliers can't be superstars in that sport!

Basketball player Anthony (Spud) Webb stood only 5'7" but averaged nearly 10 points per game over his 10+ years in the NBA. That man could *jump*!

Gymnasts, for example, are tiny. 5'5" Svetlana Khorkina was a head taller than most of her competitors, yet she won seven Olympic and twenty world championship medals.

Belgian road cycling superstar Wout van Aert has a much heavier build than many of his cycling competitors. People never thought he could win mountaintop stages since he is built like a sprinter.

They also said he couldn't "break away" from the pack and ride solo in the front, uncontested, and win a stage. Apparently, someone forgot to tell him that he was too big to climb and not aerodynamic enough to stay away from a pursuing peloton. He won several prestigious mountaintop stages in addition to the coveted sprinter's green jersey for the overall fastest sprinter in the 2022 Tour de France.

While it's an extra challenge to overcome an "atypical" body type at the elite level of any sport, it has been done, and will continue to be done by athletes who operate on pure grit.

The trick to being great at a sport you "aren't suited for" lies in being meticulous about your training, including mental training. Your skills, strategy, nutrition, mindset, and drive all have to be top-notch. Over time, training will also shape your body to align it more with the chosen sport.

Don't dwell on your height, the size of your quads, the length of your arms, or whether you're chiseled or chunky. Instead, develop "adaptive strategies" to help you compensate. 99% of the time, these strategies are mental: you're simply willing to endure more pain or discomfort and, to the extent that it's possible (and healthy!), mold your body into a shape more suited for the sport.

What you eat is one of the ways that you can make the most of your body type.

<u>What to Eat for Your Body Type</u>

All groups should eat nutrient-dense foods rich in micronutrients (vitamins and minerals), which means mostly vegetables and fruit. If you're not a veggie lover, learn how to make smoothies. You can disguise practically any vegetable in a delicious smoothie blended with bananas, apples, or berries for sweetness!

The biggest differences performance-wise lie in how much of each *macronutrient* each body type should eat. Macronutrients include carbohydrates, proteins, and fats.

The main benefit of this eating plan is that you can tweak the diet based on whether you need to lose or gain weight.

Ectomorphs eat moderate amounts of protein, low fat, and more carbohydrates than other groups. One suggested ratio is 45-35-20. Just because you can eat more carbs, however, doesn't mean junk carbs. Always look for nutrient-dense foods that will fuel your sport. Avoid high-fat/high-protein diets such as the Keto diet, which can make it even harder to put on healthy muscle weight.

Mesomorphs divide their macronutrient ratio evenly: 33-33-33 percent protein, fat, and carbohydrates. Depending on whether you need to lose weight or gain weight, you may need to *increase the fat intake and reduce carb intake* to lose weight or decrease fat intake and increase carb intake to gain weight.

Endomorphs eat carbohydrates, protein, and fat in order to stay leaner: 20-40-40. A high-protein, high-fat diet with minimal carbs, such as the Keto diet, is ideal for this body type.

How to Train for Your Body Type

Ectomorphs tend to have a fast metabolism. They need more anaerobic strength training to develop muscles and less steady-state cardio (which they are naturally good at).

Mesomorphs have it easiest: depending on the sport, you can do any type of exercise, from steady-state cardio to HIIT training.

Endomorphs should focus on HIIT training to make their metabolism "burn hotter," which will help them stay muscular yet lean.

Gender

Nutritional needs vary by gender, too.

Girls need 18mg of iron a day (due to their periods), and boys need 8mg. Deliver more oxygen to your muscles and make your brain sharper by eating iron-rich foods like spinach, beans, broccoli, meat, fish, and poultry. Iron helps make hemoglobin, a protein found in red blood cells which carry oxygen throughout the body.

Boys need more calories and protein than girls to maintain their already larger muscle mass.

Sport

The nutritional needs of sprinters, gymnasts, football players, distance swimmers, and soccer players are different. Some sports need you to be lean, while others require more mass. Athletes needing to bulk up can add a protein powder to a healthy diet. Athletes needing to trim down can boost the fat-burning process by cutting carbs and eating more fat. I know it's counterintuitive that eating more fat will make you leaner, but a high-fat/high-protein/low-carb diet will put your body in ketosis where it burns fat as fuel.

You don't need a lot of extra protein than your friends who don't do sports. Protein alone won't build muscle; that comes from strength training.

- Endurance athletes need to eat about .003 pounds of protein per pound of body weight per day. That comes to about .45 pounds for a 150-pound athlete.
- Power athletes need to eat about .004 pounds of protein per pound of body weight per day. That comes to about .6 pounds for a 150-pound athlete.

Whatever your sport, you will need either fats or carbohydrates as fuel. Carbs give you explosive energy, but the effect is short-lived. Fats give you sustained energy. The longer/more intense the sport, the more fat you'll want to eat because your muscles will quickly burn through stored glycogen.

This is key: DO NOT choose foods that mix fats and carbs unless you want to gain a lot of weight. That means ice cream should be a special treat only because it mixes fat and simple carbs!

Age

Your bones will keep growing until your 20s. Strengthen your still-growing bones with calcium-rich foods like dairy, almond milk, fish, and leafy green veggies. Boost calcium absorption by eating citrus fruits (the acid in them helps dissolve the calcium).

Nutrition Essentials

Food has so much emotion around it. It's fuel, and it can make you sleepy and dopey. It's fun, and it can cause guilt. It can be medicine, or it can be poison. It can support the growth of muscle or the growth of fat.

Let's talk about what you need as an athlete and what you can do about the not-so-good stuff.

Vitamins and Minerals

There are too many vitamins and minerals to list here. It's not accurate to say that there are two or three that you need to focus on because they're *all* important. Without going into exhaustive detail about which vitamin or mineral does what in your body, let's cut to the chase:

EAT MORE VEGETABLES!!

There is simply no better way than adding vegetables to your diet to give your body the nutritional support it needs to give you the best performance possible. Most people are deficient in their veggie intake; many athletes focus on protein but not plant-based micronutrients.

A Word on Sugar

Most teens have an insatiable sweet tooth. I know you sometimes need a quick energy gel during a workout and re-energize after a workout with a bar or banana, and that's fine. But did you know that many Americans eat 60 pounds of sugar (mostly from processed foods) every year? For some of you that's probably half your body weight! It's no wonder we're such a fat country.

You might find some "experts" saying it's okay for teens to eat around seven teaspoons of sugar a day. What they fail to tell you, however, is that plain sugar is nothing but empty calories that causes inflammation and gives you zits. Constantly eating sugar also keeps you on an energy roller coaster: you're like a hummingbird one minute and totally sloth-like the next because your body has burned through that sugar like rocket fuel. It's easy to get addicted to sugar.

Here's how to use sugar to fuel your sport:

- Eat carbs and protein immediately after a workout to replenish muscle glycogen and help muscle growth
- Get most of your sugars from fruit, which also delivers micronutrients like vitamins and minerals that your body needs to stay in top condition. Most fruits are loaded with antioxidants to support muscle recovery.

- Avoid nutritionally empty sugars: everything you put in your body either contributes to good health and athletic performance or interferes with it.

A trail mix with dried fruit and nuts is a great snack for mid-workout energy slumps as well as post-workout recovery food.

Fat

Eating fat will not make you fat. As an athlete, most of your calories should come from fat because it's the best fuel for *sustained* energy. Any kind of fat is good! New studies are showing that the low-fat/"good fat/ bad fat" movement of the last 40 years is actually false. Your body has to be fueled by something, and it's either going to be carbohydrates or fat. A low-fat diet that emphasizes high-carb intake is okay for some athletes who struggle to gain weight, but that same diet will make it really hard to lose weight if that's what you need to do.

So don't shy away from fat, and don't worry about saturated fat like butter or full-fat yogurt! Our bodies are designed to eat saturated fat. The "good fat/bad fat" rules don't apply to athletes, only to sedentary people.

Pre-Workout Nutrition

You don't need to pre-fuel with a snack if your training session is less than 45 minutes since your body will still have enough energy from previous meals.

- Eat a full meal 3-4 hours before a workout and a snack within one hour of the workout.
- Don't eat within 30 minutes of a workout because your body needs time to digest.
- A pre-workout snack should be easy to digest: high-carb, high-protein, low-fiber, and low-fat (fiber and fat are hard to digest).

The best pre-workout snacks include bananas, hash browns, oatmeal, a grilled chicken sandwich, dried fruit, Greek yogurt with berries, eggs, and trail mix.

A friend of mine swears that hash browns used to fuel her kids all the way through lunch when they went skiing!

Game-Day Eats

Your competition performance depends on the foods you've eaten over the past week. When you pay close attention to what you eat in the days leading up to competition, your body will be perfectly fueled.

- During the week leading up to the event, eat high-fat/high-protein meals.
- 3-4 hours before the event, eat a balanced meal but skip the fat because it slows digestion, and you want all of your body's resources diverted to the muscles. A high-carb, high-protein meal will fuel your event.
- Before the event, eat a light meal or snack with easy-to-digest carbs such as crackers or fruit.
- Eat within 30 minutes after the event to replenish muscles, and then again 2 hours later.
- During the event, try to minimize sugar consumption. Eat enough to keep your energy high but not so much that your stomach will rebel. Your body can't process sugar faster than 8 oz per hour; overloading your system with sugar will cause the sugars to sit in your gut, which can cause nausea, cramping, and vomiting. Small amounts, such as a carbohydrate gel pack once an hour, are plenty.
- Be sure to hydrate well on game day!

Post-Workout Nutrition

Post-workout, your main objective is to restore glycogen stores in the muscles and eat protein to help rebuild them. Post-workout snack suggestions include:

- Chocolate milk
- A protein bar and fruit
- Greek yogurt with granola and fruit
- A protein smoothie with Greek yogurt, chia seeds, fruits and veggies, and milk
- A fruit/veggie smoothie with protein powder
- A PBJ
- String cheese and fruit
- Rice cakes with nut butter and fruit
- Hummus with crackers and veggies
- Eggs
- Pasta and chicken
- Nuts and fruit

Top Athletes' Nutrition Hacks

Rebekkah Bruson, five-time WNBA champion, says — wisely — that what works for one person may not work for another. She advises young athletes to learn to listen to their bodies. You may really really want that pint of ice cream, but you ignore that it makes you feel tired and heavy afterward. What works for Rebekkah is to eat more protein and vegetables, limit carbs like pasta and bread, and she likes to enjoy occasional treats far enough from the competition so the food won't negatively affect her performance.

Tori Bowie, a world champion sprinter, advises eating most of her nutrients from fresh fruits and vegetables: fruit/veggie smoothies are a great way to stay hydrated while stocking up the body with vitamins and minerals.

Gwen Jorgensen, Olympic gold medalist in triathlon, makes the first two meals of the day more calorie-dense to fuel her day and then finishes the day with a light dinner. Breakfast may include oatmeal, peanut butter, fruit, and two eggs. She'll snack on full-fat yogurt and berries after her morning workout. Lunch may be red meat, rice, cheese, and plenty of veggies.

Rebecca Soni, a six-time Olympic medalist in swimming, likes to eat small frequent meals to avoid feeling heavy and bloated before a swim. She focuses on clean foods (natural, whole, and unprocessed), which help speed up recovery.

Emma Coburn, steeplechase world champion, advocates for eating immediately after a workout to restore glycogen in the muscles, which speeds up recovery. Her go-to foods include bananas, smoothies, or an energy bar.

Hydration

Like nutrition, everyone has unique hydration needs. Temperature, intensity, and duration of the activity, age, sex, and body composition factor into how much an athlete should drink. This means there's no one-size-fits-all formula. The best way to gauge whether you're drinking enough is the pee test: you're drinking enough if your urine is clear or almost clear. If it's dark, you're dehydrated.

Pre-workout hydration helps prep your body for activity. Start by drinking consistently for four hours before the workout. Eating salty foods will increase thirst and fluid retention. By the time you start your workout, your pee should be clear.

Hydration during exercise is, of course, essential to prevent a loss of performance. The more you sweat, the more you'll need to replenish fluids but don't let not sweating fool you. On a cross-country run in late fall, you might not sweat at all, but you're still exhaling a lot of fluid. Even if you aren't thirsty, drink steadily throughout the workout or event, *at least* 12-16 ounces every 15-20 minutes, and more if you're sweating a lot. Sports drinks are ideal for workouts lasting more than an hour because they contain carbohydrates and electrolytes.

Post-workout rehydration replaces lost electrolytes and fluids. To determine exactly how much you should drink after a workout, weigh yourself before and after. For every pound you lose during exercise, you'll need to consume around 3 cups of fluids, not all at once, but steadily until your pee is clear again.

Some of the best drinks for pre/during/post workouts include coconut water, pickle juice, water with electrolytes, fruit juice, and sports drinks. Plain water is always good, but keep in mind it won't replace lost electrolytes. Electrolyte drinks like Powerade or Gatorade are good, but beware of the high sugar content. They should be reserved for training/competition but not recovery. Plenty of recovery drink mixes on the market will refuel your muscles without the sugar hit!

What To Do If You Hate Veggies

If you don't love veggies, I recommend smoothies. A friend's son refused to eat vegetables as a kid, so every day, he had what my friend called "Swamp Juice" (what 10-year-old boy doesn't love swamp juice, right?) which was a smoothie made with apples, bananas, and various leafy greens. These smoothies taste like apple/banana sauce, but they're loaded with nutrition! By the way, her son is now a chef, so if you hate veggies, you'll probably outgrow it.

Parting Thoughts on Nutrition

Don't get too hung up on nutrition. Counting calories, grams of protein, etc., can add to an already stressful day, and it's not worth it. As long as you eat at least 80% healthy on a regular basis and your meals are balanced (the more color, the better!), you'll be fueling your body well for your sport.

Listen to your body. Really pay attention to how you feel after a meal or snack. If a meal energizes you until the next meal, eat more food like that! If it sends you into a food coma and your energy tanks two hours later, eat less food like that! You can't fuel your body on crackers alone. You need a balanced mix of macronutrients and micronutrients!

Check out all the Trackers in the companion Workbook, including hydration, nutrition, workout routine, etc.

Part of good nutrition is enlisting the help of your support network. Let's dive into the need for building a solid support network: your "Dream Team."

In the next section, we'll talk about one of the most important elements of success as an athlete: your support network, or your "dream team."

Part 3: The Dream Team

No athlete can achieve success on their own. Every athlete needs a support network or a "Dream Team" of people who are 100% behind them. Ask any elite athlete to describe their achievements; they will almost always mention the people who helped them along the way, including their coaches, families, and mentors.

"Choose to focus your time, energy and conversation around people who inspire you, support you and help you to grow you into your happiest, strongest, wisest self."

~ Karen Salmansohn, author

CHAPTER 11

BUILDING A STRONG TEAM (YOUR SUPPORT NETWORK)

"Alone, I run fast. Together, we run far."

~ African proverb

A support network consists of a group of people whose intention is to enhance the well-being of the athlete. It is important that the support network is made up of different people. This will help with seeing problems from multiple points of view, give a more complete picture of a situation, and avoid the athlete having to rely on just a few people, which can burn everyone out quickly.

In an ideal world, a support network gives a young athlete non-judgmental feedback, supports the development of skills and sportsmanship, teaches motivation and self-confidence, and helps them deal with failure, loss, and setbacks such as recovery from injury. The network supports them through their lows and celebrates their victories with them. It also provides logistical support like purchasing equipment, paying fees, and driving to and from practice and competition.

Not all athletes have a strong support network. For example, the "Bank of Mom and Dad" can usually only go so far in paying for sometimes exorbitant fees for ice time, equipment, and travel expenses. Therefore, it may be left up to the athlete to find help. I recommend finding clubs or organizations online that help develop young athletes by funding their progression through the sport. There are lots of resources online if you're resourceful!

Building this network may mean reaching outside of the immediate family or coaches. Young athletes can find support if they need it by creating a list of people they know who have skills, expertise, knowledge, resources, or contacts that can help. Most people are happy to help, so don't be shy in asking! The help can be tangible such as financial assistance or specialized skills coaching, or intangible such as guidance, an empathetic ear, or a non-judgmental sounding board.

One word of caution when it comes to a support network of friends: an athlete has to be very particular about the people they surround themselves with. Just because they've been friends with someone since kindergarten doesn't mean that this friend is supportive. Unsupportive friendships will fall away on their own as the athlete gets busy with their sport and makes friends among teammates and even competitors, but sometimes, a hard choice will have to be made.

In the next part, I offer guidelines for your "dream team" (your friends, family, and coaches) on how to best support you. Please share this book with them. Most everyone I know wants to support an athlete they know... but they don't know how to help.

In the following chapters, we'll talk directly about the key pillars of a young athlete's support network: friends, parents, and coaches.

CHAPTER 12

THE ROLE OF FRIENDS

> **"A friend is someone who makes it easy to believe in yourself."**
>
> ~ Heidi Wills, small business owner

Solid friends who support an athlete are worth their weight in gold. Abby and Luke both have one or two close friends who "get" their dedication to their sport. These friends don't try to pressure Abby or Luke into things that will hold them back, like partying or binging on junk food while studying.

Friends can help their athlete buddies train outside formal practice by introducing other activities. Ancient Greek athletes, for example, didn't have fancy gyms or expensive equipment. They just went out and did chores.

How can friends help their athlete buddies train? Hire out to do yard work for neighbors together. Walk the neighbor's dogs together. Go on hikes. Climb trees. Play backyard games like Ultimate Frisbee.

Abby, like many teen girls, is crazy about horses. Her best friend has two horses, Star and Belle. She often invites Abby to ride with her. Riding helps Abby develop different muscles and works on her balance. Sometimes Abby will even imagine that she's riding Star in a race, galloping fast, with wind in her hair and a huge smile on her face.

Luke loves video games. While many involve thumb workouts and a little more, he also enjoys some PS4 time with his friends, playing virtual sports.

Friends can also help with mental training. Be a cheerleader to your athlete friend. Let them vent when they need to, highlight their achievements and progress, help them see the lessons in failures, help them focus on "what's important now" during competition, remind them of their goals when they're down, and keep them company during downtime from injury.

Sports are ultimately about becoming the best version of yourself, and friends can be so important in supporting you. Where a parent may overlook flaws, a good friend will tell you when you're being a jerk. A good friend will understand what you feel and why you're scared.

Good friends help you see past your own limits. Sometimes, all it takes is a different perspective to get you past an obstacle!

Good Friends Will Make You Laugh

When you're at a low point and you can't get out of your head, humor can help. But it doesn't always come easily; this is where friends come in. Spend more time with friends who uplift you and make you laugh!

CHAPTER 13

THE ROLE OF PARENTS

> ## "The Golden Rule of Parenting is do unto your children as you wish your parents had done unto you!"
>
> ~ Louise Hart, psychologist/author

I'm not here to tell parents how to raise their kids. This chapter intends to support parents in discovering ways to support their kids and teach them the foundational skills of mental toughness. As a former high school athlete, I leaned heavily on my parents for support. As a mother, I strive to give my kids wings.

High school sports have changed. Coaching methods have changed. Kids have changed. It's so different now that my own kids are competitive athletes than when I was their age. I've seen my share of "soccer moms," and those toxic alpha dads who scream at coaches but most of us aren't like that. Most of us want our kids to succeed at the sport, of course, but we also want it to be a fun experience and powerful life lessons like sportsmanship, teamwork, self-discipline, and grit.

Every parent wants to believe their child will be the next Olympic gold medal holder, Superbowl champion, or world record holder. While not all kids can rise to the very top of their sports, it takes parental support to get them as far as possible, to the point where their own talents and mental toughness take them the rest of the way. Being the best sports parent is so much more than being the loudest in the stands or driving your kid to endless practices and competitions. You are where their mental toughness education starts. Are you up to the challenge?

Keep Your Cool Part 1

Sports are supposed to be fun! Parents who overreact at both wins and losses take the fun out of the sport. In fact, it's the parents' reactions that are the #1 reason kids quit sports. Avoid reaming a kid out for a missed goal or showering them with praise for something not extraordinary. Celebrate the highs and support them in the lows, but most of all, just be there. Be their rock.

Keep Your Cool Part 2

Sports are supposed to be fun! Coaches and umpires are there for the love of the sport and to develop all athletes, not to make your kid look good or to discipline your kid. If your child is being rude and disrespectful, then discipline is in order, but it has to come from you. If your child is benched or the umpire calls a foul, show the kids by example how to handle a conflict with self-control and grace.

Don't Hover: Let Them Spread Their Wings

Don't come to practice but try to be there at every competition. Kids act differently when their parents are present. They will probably be more reserved and less likely to try new things or make new friends. Helicopters are great for news coverage, but coaches and kids always feel like they're under a microscope when helicopter parents won't give them space. The parents who live vicariously through their kids put *so much pressure* on the child. My advice? Remember that sports are supposed to be fun. Let your kid be a kid.

Above all, don't act like a search and rescue helicopter every time your child gets in a bind. I get it, it's so hard not to want to rescue your kids when they're struggling, but this will only reinforce helplessness and reliance on mommy and daddy. Letting kids learn through natural consequences is the most powerful way to give them a solid foundation as athletes and young adults.

Your child should pack their own bags, do their own laundry, and schedule their free time. Personal responsibility is a life skill that sports teach so well. Let them learn.

Keep Sports Fun

I keep repeating that sports are supposed to be fun, only because it's so easy to forget. We get caught up in the excitement, and our emotions can go just as high and devastatingly low as the athletes' emotions. Encourage your young athlete to view sports as play, not "practice." Just like I don't like the term "workout," because why would I want to cram more work into my already busy day? Today's kids are expected to live regimented lives where they bounce from one supervised activity to another, to the point they never have a chance to learn how to cope with boredom (they never learn to self-entertain), never learn self-regulation, organization, or time management, and rarely get to explore a sport just for fun.

One of the ways that parents ruin sports for their kids is by expecting perfection. That's an awfully high bar. High expectations are healthy, but if they're unreasonable, kids will quickly stop trying if they feel they can never measure up. Their self-confidence and self-esteem will also take a hit. Help your child set realistic goals and encourage personal excellence: simply doing their best.

One thing my husband does with our son in tackle football is he rates/grades him at the end of practice. A: Great effort/coachable. Listened to the coach. B: Pretty good effort, could do better. C: Average effort, some good moments, but a handful of off-task moments and not trying as hard as he could. D: More off-task moments, sad, tears, not coachable, not into the practice. F: Lots of tears, not finishing workouts/training. Not coachable. Poor sport. Not a team player.

Then, invite your athlete to grade themselves. This is an excellent self-reflection time. Try this grading system and let me know if it worked/didn't work.

Try this grading system and let me know if it worked/didn't work.

Explore Other Sports

Many kids play just one sport, hoping that specializing in one will make them better at it. This isn't always the case. Just like you need cross-training to work different types of muscles, kids need different sports to teach them different skills.

Strength and Conditioning Specialist Elsbeth Vaino says that 82% of the top professional athletes in the Big Four major sports in the USA (football, baseball, basketball, and hockey played more than one sport.

Explore Other Activities Outside of Sports

This one is hard but incredibly valuable. With the already hectic schedules that many kids have, it's hard to balance school, athletics, social life, and now yet another thing. Well, hear me out. *That's a pretty privileged life!* What about a part-time job to help pay for sports equipment? What about chores? What about volunteering at the local animal shelter or soup kitchen to give kids an appreciation for what they have? Even an hour a week doing something completely unrelated to school or sports can help make a child more well-rounded.

The value of chores teaches kids several important things. One: a job isn't done until it's done (which teaches kids to be task-oriented and not time-oriented). Two: the family is a team, so do your part. Three: chores teach a child to be proud of his or her efforts. Half-assed efforts carry through to adulthood and jobs, with not-great consequences.

Teach Them to Lose Well

Losing is a part of life, but that doesn't mean that kids should learn that it's okay to lose. Yes, losing can be a valuable lesson, but not if a child gets used to losing and everyone being okay with it. No! The fire of excellence needs to be lit. The lessons that come from losing should be hard lessons because, although the loss may sting now, the consequences of losing should build resilience and teach life skills. *Whoever came up with participation trophies... we need to have a word!*

Sports are like life on a more controlled and smaller scale. Kids get cut from the team, and they lose — and it doesn't make them victims. Life is unfair, and while sports are meant to be fair, there will be instances of bad calls or biased scores. Rather than blaming others and letting your child play the victim, encourage your child to turn rejection, failure, and disappointment into strength.

Remember that any time you lay blame on others for your child's loss, it's only fair that you also give credit to others when your child wins.

Don't Brag About Your Child

Tell your child you're proud of his/her achievements, how they overcame challenges, how hard they work, and how far they've come. But don't brag to the other parents or the coaches, because there's an inverse relationship between how much a parent brags and how talented and hardworking a child actually is. Even if your child is at the top of their game and headed for the elite level, keep them grounded.

Introduce your child as a competitor or an athlete, not as a "star" or a "winner." That not only puts tremendous pressure on the child, but doesn't acknowledge the fact that they won't always be stars or winners.

A funny story: a friend's daughter was visibly embarrassed that her parents were by far the loudest parents in the stands. We're talking many decibels louder than the rest of the spectators. My friend leaned over to the girl and said, "Well, no wonder you're so fast. Now I know where you get your lungs!" The girl immediately cracked a huge grin. Sometimes all it takes is a shift in perspective to make a child feel empowered instead of embarrassed!

Teach Sportsmanship

Teach sportsmanship so your child understands the true spirit of sport: not "crushing their opponents" but rather "crushing their own inner limits."

- Making eye contact and giving a firm handshake
- Sending thank-you notes
- Knowing how to apologize
- Speaking respectfully about others, especially opponents
- Taking full responsibility for the outcome
- Celebrating other people's successes
- Holding themselves accountable and following through on promises
- Owning their mistakes
- Being enthusiastic and encouraging with teammates
- Handling conflict maturely
- Handling defeat with grace and not quitting because of defeat
- Being positive
- Being grateful and appreciative of the help that others have given them (coaches, you, opponents, teachers, peers, mentors, etc.)
- Finding the benefits in defeat
- Knowing that compassion and honesty are more

important than winning at all costs
- Always doing their best

Never, ever give participation trophies or celebrate what's expected (i.e., not giving them a pass on household chores just for showing up to practice).

Teach Resilience

Lead by example. Kids learn resilience through observation: monkey see, monkey do. Resilient kids do much better in life than those who have learned to play the victim card. They know how to empower themselves with positive self-talk. They set boundaries and know when to say no. They adapt to change, own their mistakes, and keep going no matter what.

Mistakes, handled right, teach resilience. Mistakes are not wrong; they are a necessary step to success. How many times does a baby pull herself up, take a few wobbly steps, and whumps to the ground on her butt? Is she a failure for not walking immediately? Of course not! Let your kids make mistakes and teach them that mistakes are part of life! Don't bail them out. Let them experience natural consequences. They will be embarrassed — let them! Embarrassment won't kill them. Embarrassment is a great teacher. Don't shield a young athlete from life and its pain, fear, disappointment, embarrassment, frustration, or other "negative" emotions. Joy can't be experienced fully without also understanding sadness. You can't fully taste the sweetness of winning if you don't know what losing feels like.

Encourage healthy self-talk (there's a section on that in the young athlete's section; I recommend you to read it).

Teach Emotional Self-Mastery

Emotional self-mastery doesn't mean "stuff your emotions down." None of that stiff-upper-lip nonsense. Don't minimize, ignore, or deny their emotions or make them feel bad for having them. Instead, teach children that it's okay to feel emotions but that emotions are temporary and not necessary to act on them. Usually, negative emotions are tied to losing or making mistakes. Help your child understand that these are valuable lessons.

Teach them gratitude for the hard things in life. Eventually, if the child even remembers the event, they will remember it fondly as a turning point or the day that they had a major revelation.

Teach your child how to face their fears one step at a time, and they'll grow up being able to get out of their comfort zone and take action in spite of their fears.

Teach your child impulse control and self-discipline: these two skills, along with facing fears, will help them achieve any goal they have in sports, school, and beyond.

Teach them not to crumble when faced with a problem.

I like to use the analogy of water. When faced with an obstacle, water finds a way around, over, or through.

Encourage your child to visualize themselves flowing like water over an obstacle, around it, or, more forcefully, through it.

Don't tell an angry child to calm down because that minimizes their feelings. Don't try to cheer them up every time they're sad. They need to learn how to feel and deal with emotions. You won't always be there to regulate their moods, and there will be plenty of times they will need to self-soothe in training and competition. Show them how, but don't do it for them.

Teach Perseverance

Many parents let their kids quit a sport at the first sign of trouble. While you've got to tread a fine line between making a child fulfill a commitment they made and completely sucking the joy out of their lives, mentally tough athletes always learn to persevere.

When I was in 3rd grade, I wanted to quit dance. I was not a great dancer, and my friends were all much better. I felt like I was in the wrong sport and wasn't loving it anymore. My wise mother told me to at least finish the season through the recital. Well, I ended up loving the recital and had a great time! I fell in love with dance again and went on to be a NBA Denver Nugget Dancer and traveled literally around the world with my dance skills. I am forever grateful to my wonderful momma!

Support Their Dreams; Don't Push Them Into Yours

I can't tell you how many overzealous football dads and dance moms are out there (totally stereotyping here, but you get the picture) living vicariously through their kids, pushing them toward greatness in a sport the parents love, and totally ignoring the child's interests or desires. Kids aren't mini-me's. They are their own people with their own dreams.

Talk about your own goals and show your child what you're doing to make those goals happen. Show them that you prioritize constant improvement. Use the companion Workbook to help your child log and dialogue, and journal all of the ideas they're learning in this book.

Teach Them Personal Responsibility

This goes hand in hand with integrity. If you say you're going to do something, do it. You can allow them to explain why something didn't get done but do not tolerate excuses. Don't allow your child to play the blame game. Even if people or events conspired against them, the individual always has the final choice in what to say or do.

Be There. Be Their Rock.

A child's physical safety is important, of course, but so is their emotional/psychological safety. If they come to you with a problem, fear, disappointment, or hurt, listen. Be there for them. Teach them autonomy by helping them navigate difficult situations, but don't do everything for them.

CHAPTER 14

THE ROLE OF COACHES

"The key is not the will to win.
Everybody has that. It is the
will to prepare to win that is
important."

~ Bobby "the General" Knight, former
basketball coach

I'm not here to tell coaches how to coach. The intent of this chapter is to support coaches in discovering ways to connect with kids and use mental toughness techniques that have only just now begun trickling down to high school sports.

Let's tackle the biggest misconception about mental toughness: that it can only be taught by brutal methods. Old-school coaches would beat mental toughness into their athletes, sometimes to the point of serious damage to the athlete's mental health. If an athlete was struggling, perhaps because of family troubles, it was equated with "not trying hard enough." While boot-camp tactics might work in the military, they definitely don't have a place in high school sports.

Advanced mental toughness training for high school athletes focuses on encouraging them — not berating them — to continue to do their best regardless of what happens inside or outside of training or competition.

Making the Most of Practice

A young athlete's coach is different from an adult coach. Kids are growing in fits and spurts; their hormones are all over the place, and they are just getting to know their bodies, and those bodies are changing every day. High school athletes are crossing the bridge from dependent children to independent adults.

A gradual approach to developing high school athletes is often the best approach. This requires some knowledge about child development and how teenagers are neither children nor adults. They have different needs for recovery, building strength and endurance, and the mental game.

You Can't Rush Or Change a Developing Body

Kids grow and develop at different speeds according to their own biological clock. Just because someone's calendar age is 15 doesn't mean their musculature is as developed as a kid on the team who's just 13. Focus on what the athletes can do, and allow their bodies to mature enough to develop the power, coordination, speed, strength, and endurance they need. One thing is for sure: they are never too young to focus on training their minds.

Many kids grow in spurts. They literally have to relearn how to move their suddenly larger bodies. Bones grow faster than muscles, which disrupts coordination, speed, and strength. The resulting decrease in performance can leave everyone feeling frustrated. Once again, you can focus on their mental game when they're going through a growth spurt. Soon enough, they'll mature into their new bodies!

Female athletes who are on their menstrual cycle are losing a lot of iron. This makes their muscles less efficient. They don't need more intense training during this time. They need less intensity. They will likely not share that they're on their period. Observation is important. Knowing your athletes and when they're "off" can help you tailor training to their cycle. There's simply no way around it. Overtraining during a menstrual cycle can lead to sleep disturbances and fatigue, which affect not only the sport but school as well.

Overuse injuries are much more common when a young athlete is going through a growth spurt. Good core strength will minimize poor biomechanics that lead to injury. Dynamic isometric training is the best way to develop core strength in adolescents. Forget crunches! No sport uses them in its movements, and they can lead to muscle strength imbalance and even low back pain. The Plank Bird Dog (raising the opposite arm and leg while in plank) takes the conventional plank to the next level while developing incredible core stability.

Think about this: if your physical balance is off, so is your whole life. Just as the mind influences the body, the body influences the mind. Encourage your child to work on balance. It will help them with their athletic form, explosive power, and injury prevention.

Also, consider each athlete's training age. A 16-year-old who has only been doing weight training since the beginning of the season will have different needs and expectations than a 16-year-old who has been weight training for several years — even if that first 16-year-old is bigger and stronger, she may need to start with, for example, bodyweight-only single leg deadlifts rather than the more advanced kettlebell single leg deadlifts.

Encouraging Behavioral Changes

Kids hate to be lectured. They get enough of that from parents and teachers. They are smart, sneaky little manipulative geniuses (said with pure love — they do whatever works). When it comes to healthy behavior like snacking that will support their athletic goals, it's up to you to model the behavior you want to see. Walk the talk.

Goal Setting

Setting SMART goals helps keep kids accountable and tracks their progress. This is hugely motivational since the goals are achievable with a little extra effort but not so grand that they seem impossible. Regular progress reports help fine-tune the training of the individual athlete.

Meet kids where they are. Take into account their biological age, developmental age, and training age.

Free Play

High school athletes' training regimens are pretty structured. Free play is essential for developing their nervous system. A simple game of tag can release tension and relax kids who are under a lot of pressure to perform.

The Art of Motivation
Everyone responds differently to the following motivational theories. Your challenge is to find what motivates each individual athlete.

Instinct Theory

Motivation comes from evolutionary programming when competition ensures survival: whoever hunts down the herd first gets to eat while the competition starves. This theory is rarely talked about in sports psychology because sports are meant to be fun, not win/survive or lose/die. However, there is something "primal" about competing against others, something that drives athletes to greater effort, as Norman Triplett observed in 1898.

Drive Theory

Motivation comes from meeting unmet needs. You are motivated to eat when you're hungry. The need remains unmet, and therefore the drive remains strong until you eat something. While we do sports for fun, not because we need to, there's still an unmet desire, whether it's a desire for a prize or the satisfaction of shattering your PR (personal record).

Arousal Theory

Motivation comes from a desire to reach a certain level of arousal. Training stimulates the release of endorphins, serotonin, and dopamine (the "feel good" hormones), and you feel more stimulated/excited/aroused; on the flip side, meditation or reading promotes relaxation and calm. This relates to sports in that we are motivated by pleasure. While sports can hurt, they also feel incredibly good, and we want more of that feeling.

Humanistic Theory

Motivation comes from the brain: there are cognitive reasons for staying motivated. Abraham Maslow's "Hierarchy of Needs," which describes how we need to tend to our basic needs first before fulfilling "higher" needs, such as fulfilling one's potential, explains this. Many high school athletes have the time and resources to devote to fulfilling their athletic potential, but others don't and must juggle after-school jobs and difficult family situations. Their drive to change their circumstances can be incredibly strong.

Expectancy Theory

Motivation comes from how you imagine a future outcome. If you imagine yourself on the podium, you will be more motivated to push harder in those early morning workouts than if you imagine yourself in the top 100. The more you believe in and expect an imagined future outcome, the more you will do what it takes to make it a reality.

Incentive Theory

Motivation comes from extrinsic (external) rewards such as medals, championship status, or even sponsorship, or from intrinsic (internal) rewards such as personal satisfaction, the joy of overcoming, and other positive feelings that come from the process and the achievement. The greater the perceived extrinsic or intrinsic reward, the greater the motivation.

Focus On the 4 C's of Mental Toughness

Mental toughness can be distilled into four elements: control, challenge, commitment, and confidence.

Control/Composure

Control refers to self-control: blocking out distractions, staying focused, and managing emotions. All athletes get angry, upset, or frustrated with themselves after making a mistake. Just as the mind influences the body, the body influences the mind. Have the athlete use their body to redirect their mind away from the mistake toward what they need to do next.

- Stand tall with head up, shoulders back, eyes forward
- Breathe deeply to calm down
- Smile to signal to the brain that "this is okay, nothing to panic about."
- Say to yourself, "Okay, that happened. Moving on."

This simple technique can help keep an athlete from becoming rattled and avoid sulking or quitting.

Visualization/Mental Rehearsal

The mind is everything in sports. Encourage athletes to mentally rehearse success as well as to imagine themselves overcoming every conceivable obstacle. The key to successful visualization is to feel emotions, which are the true drivers of behaviors.

Challenge

Challenge is the ability to perceive threats as opportunities. Challenges can include particularly strong competitors, being in last place, bad weather, training setbacks like injury, or persistent negative thoughts. The key to facing challenges is to become resilient and adaptable and to practice mental rehearsal.

Help Them Cope with Injury

One of the biggest challenges athletes face is coping with injury. Many are angry, sad, and afraid that they will, at the very least, lose their edge. Encourage the athlete to practice mental rehearsal and follow their recovery instructions rigorously to avoid returning to play before their body is ready.

Help Them See Setbacks and Failures as Opportunities

Mentally tough players see failures and setbacks as opportunities to learn and grow. Giving critical feedback in a way that's encouraging will help athletes learn from their mistakes and bounce back from losses. Athletes know when they have made a mistake. Encourage them to move on, trust their training, and confidently take the next shot or run the next race.

Model Appropriate Responses to Challenges

Set the tone for your athletes by modeling and mimicking championship-level verbal and non-verbal communication in the face of a challenge. Do you get tense and uptight when the team is losing in the third quarter, or do you welcome the challenge as an opportunity to help your team up-level their game? When your athletes see that you remain calm and composed no matter what, they will unconsciously mimic that attitude. Show your athletes that you trust them to do their best because you know (and they know) they are prepared.

In any competition or any season, there will be ups and downs. Some years, your athletes may all be at the top of their game and the next, they're the lowest-scoring team in the league. This natural ebb and flow is a good way to teach mental toughness: don't lose focus or enthusiasm when you're in an ebb period. Continue encouraging them to do their very best, knowing that a flow period will come.

Commitment

Commitment is what athletes do every day. They show up, train, and stay focused during competition. Setting the right goals helps athletes stay committed.

Use the Power of Routine

Develop your athlete's pre-play routines that "automate" skills like a golf shot, pitch, serve, free throw, dismount, or turn. The physical part of a routine is often easy to implement: it can include, for example, bouncing the ball three times; tapping the knee three times; several fast, forceful exhales; or tapping the ground with a racquet. During this time, the athlete is also mentally rehearsing the move.

Check out the trackers inside the companion Workbook.

Measure Progress

Measuring progress can demonstrate to an athlete that he or she is becoming tougher as their goals get tougher.

Stick to the Plan

Commitment is important when nothing is going as planned. Remind your athletes of their goals, and commit to the plan whether they're leading or in last place. Demonstrate your commitment to them and they will respond in kind. Stay in the moment. Instead of overreacting to a mistake or a bad call, remain calm and positive. This demonstrates that you have moved on and that what matters is the next move, not what just happened.

Make Practice Intentional

Intentional practice means that every move, drill, or rep has a purpose. Instead of just doing the same move over and over — practice makes permanent, not necessarily perfect — helps the athlete focus on how this skill sets the foundation for more advanced skills.

Plyometrics, for example, should focus on quality (doing the movements correctly and precisely) rather than quantity. Kids who are growing into their bodies need to master them, not exhaust them.

Put As Much Emphasis on Mental Training As On Physical Training

Mental toughness has to be developed, especially in kids who are more timid or anxious. I remember starting and ending some practices with a five-minute visualization session. Giving your kids some self-talk cues before practice can help them adopt empowering self-talk.

Confidence

If athletes do not have confidence in themselves, there is no hope of winning. Fortunately, self-confidence can be taught. Letting athletes make mistakes without repercussions but as a learning process, will give them the courage to try. Kids know when you believe in them and if you do, their confidence and performance will improve. Encouraging athletes and giving them the freedom to make mistakes will grow their confidence.

The Galatea Effect and the Pygmalion Effect

The Galatea Effect states that athletes will perform better if they believe in their abilities. The Pygmalion Effect states that if you believe in your athletes, they will believe in themselves.

Teach empowering self-talk, and always use encouraging language when talking about mistakes, wins, progress, and losses.

Cry In the Dojo, Laugh in Battle

No, this doesn't mean it's okay to make your athletes cry. The point behind this ancient Japanese saying is that training — training to win — should be more demanding and challenging than the competition. Athletes gain confidence from knowing that they have developed their skills enough to perform well.

- The Practice Mindset is the one where they are focused on improving their skills.
- The Competition Mindset is the one where they trust their training, and play intuitively in the Zone.

Analyze the Replay

Make use of video. For example, you can analyze a football game and show a player getting up after a hard hit (or not); pushing through fatigue (or giving in); staying focused after a bad call (or getting frustrated and losing focus); trying again after a missed opportunity (or just going through the motions). Point out when the athlete was mentally tough, and when he wasn't.

Identify situations when an athlete maintained their performance standards despite adversity and when they didn't. Create training situations that focus on the athlete's problem areas to help them develop confidence.

Help Them W I N

To achieve peak performance, athletes must focus on the moment, not what happened in the past or what might happen in the future. For example, dwelling on a mistake can affect their next move; or worrying about future outcomes, such as fear of missing a penalty shot will also pull their focus away from what they need to do next. Only "What is important now" matters: this is the W I N strategy.

- Have athletes ask themselves, "What's important now?" It's not the game. It's the next kick, the next stroke, the next jump, the next hurdle. Have your athletes write W I N on their water bottle or on their hand so that they are constantly reminded to focus on what's important right now.
- Where the eyes go, the mind goes. Teach athletes to direct their focus to something directly related to W I N.
- Teach athletes to use neutral focus words related to the next move: *Smooth. Power. Light. Fast. Sprint. Explode. Hold. Push. Balance. Spring. Trust.* Two or three words repeated like a mantra help calm and focus the mind.
- Breathwork can help them focus on the present. Teach athletes to calm themselves and focus by simply paying attention to the experience of breathing for a minute or two.

Help Them Perform Under Pressure and Manage Expectations

Great athletes have developed the ability to consistently perform at their peak when they're under pressure. Expectations from coaches, teammates, parents, and fans can be a huge distraction. Their confidence can erode when they fail to live up to expectations. Encourage athletes to focus on doing their best, not achieving any milestone (scoring 10 points in a game, beating their PR (personal record) by 2 seconds, etc.).

Support Mental Health: Have More Fun

Use positive self-talk strategies, visualization, body language, stress relief, and anger management to help young athletes cope with the immense pressures they're under.

Many of us grew up with coaches who used boot camp-style methods like screaming at their athletes or making them run until they threw up. We now know that this is not the way to drive performance. It's a form of mental abuse!

Thankfully, those methods are falling out of favor. The key is to develop a relationship with your athletes where they expect you to be tough, critical, and demanding, but at the same time, someone they can trust because:

- You know that training hard in practice makes competition that much easier
- Your criticism is delivered in a way that is empowering
- You demand only one thing: the athlete's best effort

One great tactic is to tell your athletes to "go out there and have more fun than your competition." A young athlete just out there having a blast will be more in the Zone than an athlete who is tense and anxious.

And always be there for them if they need to talk.

The Best Pre-Competition Speech You Can Give
The pre-competition speech doesn't necessarily motivate your athletes. But it serves an important purpose: releasing pent-up tension! Not all athletes need or want a pep talk before an event. Your goal

is to read your athletes and put them in the right mindset for competition. A winning speech is short and all about them. Build excitement and a sense of fun. I keep going back to "go out there and have more fun than your competition" because it's so different from the usual "go out there and win one for the school" speech which puts so much pressure on them. Having fun doesn't come with pressure, and relaxed athletes often perform better.

The Big Don'ts of Coaching

Coaching has evolved. Based on my own experience and a deep dive into modern coaching methods, here's what to avoid as a coach:

Don't Get Visibly Upset... Be Enthusiastic

Back to the coaches who scream at kids... coaches who are overly intense and competitive tend to get emotional. I get it, your passion for the sport is showing, and you're frustrated that a child isn't giving his or her all. However, losing your cool is counterproductive. If you yell at a young athlete, they're first going to wonder why they're there (I know, I've been there). After all, you're teaching mental mastery, so model that behavior.

In competition *and* in training, be excited and energetic! Be animated! Be passionate! It shows you're invested in the sport and in your athletes' success.

Don't Point Out Mistakes By Pointing Out What They Did/Didn't Do

It's done with the best of intentions, but telling an athlete that they "didn't follow through" or "didn't lift your knees high enough" is nowhere near as effective as asking, "Why do you think you [missed the kick, botched the landing, etc.]?" Asking them, "If you could relive that [play, routine, race, etc.], what would you do differently?" encourages them to come up with a solution instead of always being told what to do, which many kids bristle at. Most of the time, they're very aware of what they did. Asking leading questions like this helps them internalize what happened and what not to do next time.

Don't Be Stuck in Old School

Sports evolve over time. Today's gymnastics is a far cry from gymnastics in the 70s. While most methods and techniques still apply, you have to adapt when the style of play changes because of new equipment (such as carbon fiber tennis racquets as opposed to wood racquets). Keep evolving with the sport. Find fresh new ways to build skills instead of relying on outdated skills.

Don't Over-Coach

A lot of the time, less is more. There's a time and place for repetition, but at some point, you've got to shut up and just watch so your athletes can demonstrate whether they've absorbed the lesson or not. Some sports, such as diving or tennis, require intense concentration, not always having the coach "in their ear." The less you say, the more meaning your words will have.

Don't Coach Everyone the Same Way

Every athlete is different. Some need a soft, more cerebral approach, while others need to be challenged to their limits. Most kids need a little of both. Take the time to get to know your athletes so you can nurture them, push them, and inspire them according to who they are.

Parting Thoughts

The best way for coaches to teach mental toughness is to demonstrate it. You can't expect your athletes not to crumble when they're behind if you show them you've given up. We're all works in progress! I encourage any coach to remember that just because you've achieved a level of expertise in a sport doesn't mean there's no room for self-improvement.

And above all, remind the kids they're here to have fun.

GO OUT THERE AND HAVE MORE FUN THAN YOUR COMPETITION!

"The only one who can tell you 'you can't win' is you, and you don't have to listen." ~ Jessica Ennis-Hill, track and field athlete

In ancient Greece, sports were not just about entertainment or fitness; it was about aspiration and what it meant to be Greek. As Socrates put it: "What a disgrace it is for a man to grow old without ever seeing the beauty and strength of which his body is capable! To develop his beauty and his strength to the utmost is the duty of a citizen."

So, the next time you go to the gym or do some exercise, always remember to be virtuous, try to read some geometry or astronomy, and lift the closest large animal you have to hand.

You have what it takes to be successful. Success in athletics comes down to "brains over brawn."

As Luke finishes up his senior year, he has his eyes set on the challenge of collegiate swimming. He knows that his high school years have prepared him well and he's excited to swim against new competitors who will push him to even greater efforts.

Luke's parting words sum up the spirit of this book: "Always bet on yourself."

Abby is looking forward to shaving more time off her personal records. She's also playing with the idea of making a move to the cross-country team, just out of curiosity to see if it would be a better fit.

Abby leaves you with her second-favorite quote, "There's just no telling how far I'll go" (Moana, the main character from the film Moana)

I have shared the experiences of Luke and Abby to help you see that regular kids can become mentally tough athletes. They take mental training as seriously as they take physical training, and their results show it.

You've learned what it means to be mentally tough and how to develop mental toughness. Now, it's up to you to practice what you've learned. Believe in yourself. Always tie everything you do back to your Why. Always do your best, no matter what. Commit.

Be disciplined. And always decide to have more fun than anyone else.

Some of the steps outlined here will be easy — maybe they're already a part of your everyday training. Some will be challenging. But let me assure you: when you train your mind, you will be absolutely unstoppable in anything you do athletically and academically. High school sports help prepare you for success in life.

But enough theory!!! Theory is meaningless until it's put into practice.

You can make much faster progress in developing mental toughness if you take the time to use the companion Workbook. It's practical, and you'll see exactly how to build mental toughness through mental rehearsal, self-talk, and yep, some probing questions.

I'm so honored that you decided to take this journey with me.

You see, I was never the best dancer. In fact, many were much better than I was. I worked hard. I trained hard. I really wanted to do great things in my mind. I persevered. I just. Kept. Going. Going to dance class. Going to high school dance team rehearsals. Going there in my mind that I can do hard things. My parents were tough on me but showed lots of love and compassion. I am so grateful for my parents. I didn't make Captain of the team. I didn't get the solo part. I wanted those things. That was a huge struggle for me. I wanted to be the best. I wanted everyone to be so proud of me. I yearned to be recognized. I never felt that in high school. I never felt "good enough."

BUT. Guess who went on to dance in college and became the President of her team senior year? Guess who went on to dance semi-professionally and then professionally with the NBA? Guess who was chosen to lead the dancers in Paris, France, in the New Year's parade? Guess who helped with the Denver Broncos halftime show retiring number 7, John Elway? Guess who got to be the guest judge for various State dance/cheer competitions? Alaska. Hawaii. Idaho. Texas. Colorado. Utah. Yep. Pretty amazing. Some pretty cool traveling gigs. How? Why?

I hope and pray you take the skills and strategies

taught in this book so you, too, can do amazing things.

You can do hard things.

You just have to believe in yourself.

Please take a moment to give me a favorable review on Amazon!

ARE YOU READY TO UNLEASH YOUR INNER CHAMPION?

COMING SOON
More Books You'll Love!

Stay up to date with new releases
Linktr.ee/AJKikumoto
Join our Facebook Group:
Mental Toughness for Elite Athletes Academy

It is my hope that after reading "Mental Toughness for Athletes" you're starting to feel empowered to help your athlete be strong and achieve more.

I need your help bringing this to more readers who are struggling with the same challenges. I would be incredibly grateful if you could take just 60 seconds to write a brief review on Amazon, even if it's just a sentence or two.

A. Kindly leave a favorable review

Scan the above QR code
Click on the book link
Skip to #4 OR

1. Log into your Amazon account.
2. Click on Your Account (3 lines)
3. Click on Your Orders: Click on the purchase of this book
4. Scroll to the bottom of the page to Customer Reviews
5. Leave a Favorable Review.
    Bonus points for sharing a Video/Photo in the Review.

B. Join our Facebook Group

Mental Toughness for
Elite Athletes Academy

Thank you!

ABOUT THE AUTHOR

AJ Kikumoto is a dance instructor and coach at Starstruck Academy of Dance in Denver, CO. A former NBA Denver Nugget Dancer (YES, World Champs!!), CBA Idaho Hot Shots Dancer and Boise State University Mane Line Dance Team President.

Mother of 6 children – 5 girls and 1 boy; All are competitive athletes involved in many sports, including basketball, football, golf, lacrosse, dance, volleyball, gymnastics, and tennis, to name a few. Their oldest dances for Texas Tech Pom Squad and recently went viral as the "Masters Girl." She and her husband coach many of these sports, and being in the trenches, saw a need for this book, "Mental Toughness for Athletes: 7 Proven Strategies for Young Champions to Build Grit, Boost Emotional Resilience and Become Unstoppable.".

AJ Kikumoto is a Marquis Who's Who, where individuals profiled are selected on factors such as position, noteworthy accomplishments, visibility, and prominence in a field.

She is the CEO of Queen Publishing Agency, which helps budding authors publish their books.

Having entered business for herself due to her own struggles in finding a publisher, Ms. Kikumoto wrote her first book series, "Zoey's Great Adventures™," in collaboration with her six children. Based on actual events, Zoey's Great Adventures™ book series teaches morals and values; every book ends with "You can do hard things," empowering young children to be their best selves and be kind to others. Aaliyah Kikumoto™ Dare 2 Dream book series recently debuted from her daughter going viral at The Masters Golf Tournament as the "Masters Girl." Coloring books, cookbooks, and journals are available now, and many more will be debuting soon.

The series seeks to raise awareness regarding Childhood Apraxia of Speech (CAS,) a speech disorder. Four of Ms. Kikumoto's children were born with CAS and were mute until they were four. She donates a portion of the proceeds to the non-profit Apraxia Kids.

In 2022 and 2023, Ms. Kikumoto was a guest speaker empowering parents to advocate for their Apraxia Star at the Apraxia Kids National Conference. The organization supports the lives of children afflicted with apraxia of speech. She also volunteers with the organization and helps with fundraising through Walk for Apraxia. Besides her effort in support of CAS, she often volunteers with the Backpack Society in Highlands Ranch, Colorado, walks to support autism, breast cancer, leukemia, and lymphoma, and is active with Feed the 5,000 through The Church of Jesus Christ of Latter-day Saints.

RESOURCES

Lee Crust & Peter J. Clough (2011) Developing Mental Toughness: From Research to Practice, Journal of Sport Psychology in Action, 2:1, 21-32, DOI: 10.1080/21520704.2011.563436

Robert Weinberg (2013) Mental toughness: What is it and how to build it, Revista da Educação Física/UEM 24(1):1-10, DOI: 10.4025/reveducfis.v24.1.17523

Laura Purcell et al (2013), Sport nutrition for young athletes, Paediatr Child Health. doi: 10.1093/pch/18.4.200

THE DYNAMOGENIC FACTORS IN PACEMAKING AND COMPETITION By Norman Triplett, 1898
https://sites.google.com/site/socialfacilitationappsych8/business-website-services

Sport Psychology, 2008, American Psychological Association
https://www.apa.org/ed/graduate/specialize/sports

Sports Psychology: Mindset Can Make or Break an Athlete, 2018, Oklahoma Wesleyan University
https://www.okwu.edu/news/2018/07/sports-psychology-make-or-break/

If you need help NOW, please call 988
(suicide and crisis hotline)
or 1800-273-8255 (national suicide prevention hotline).

Made in the USA
Coppell, TX
07 September 2023

21313761R00136